DEEPLY ROOTED

Knowing Self, Growing in God

CHRISTOPHER MARICLE

UPPER ROOM BOOKS®
NASHVILLE

Cover design: Bruce Gore | Gore Studio, Inc.
Interior design and typesetting: Kristin Goble | PerfecType

Library of Congress Cataloging-in-Publication Data

Names: Maricle, Christopher, 1963– author.
Title: Deeply rooted : knowing self, growing in God / Christopher Maricle.
Description: Nashville : Upper Room Books, 2016. | Includes bibliographical references.
Identifiers: LCCN 2016005514| ISBN 9780835815635 (print) | ISBN 9780835815642
    (mobi) | ISBN 9780835815659 (epub)
Subjects: LCSH: Spiritual formation.
Classification: LCC BV4511 .M29 2016 | DDC 248.4—dc23
LC record available at http://lccn.loc.gov/2016005514

To the memory of
Anne Hamill Maricle—

daughter of deep faith,
strong and patient wife,
devoted mother,
trusted friend,
compassionate soul to strangers.
You touched so many lives with your grace.
We will always miss you.

CONTENTS

ACKNOWLEDGMENTS

This book has been percolating for many years, and during that time, a number of "coincidences" conspired to bring the tree of the soul to my life. I was first introduced to the insights of Anthony de Mello (1931–1987) as a young teacher in 1986. Years later, I found his book *Awareness: The Perils and Opportunities of Reality*, and in 2009, I received *The Way to Love: The Last Meditations of Anthony de Mello* as a Christmas gift. De Mello's thoughts on attachments and the nature of love are simple, powerful, and easy to understand, yet require a lifetime of discipline.

In 2010, I attended a retreat conducted by Deacon Red Cheever, which expanded my ideas about faith and prayer. Cheever first introduced me to the work of Raimon Panikkar (1918–2010). Later, my wife, Anne, gave me a copy of Panikkar's last work, *The Rhythm of Being: The Unbroken Trinity*. His insights into the nature of God, reality, and freedom were invaluable. I will never be smart enough to understand fully the wisdom of this spiritual giant, "yet even the dogs eat the crumbs that fall from their masters' table" (Matt. 15:27).

In 2011, an accident of grace put the book *Clear Leadership: Sustaining Real Collaboration and Partnership at Work* by Gervase R. Bushe into my hands. His thoughts on the nature of experience helped me explore Catherine of Siena's ideas on self-knowledge.

ACKNOWLEDGMENTS

Finally, I might not have finished writing this book without my wife, Anne's, unending support and encouragement. Sarah and Nicholas, my now teenaged children, have shown remarkable patience and understanding and have listened far longer than any parent would have predicted or rightfully expected.

FROM THE DESK OF
CATHERINE OF SIENA

In his ministry, Jesus uses a lot of metaphors. Two thousand plus years later, some of the images Jesus employs are not as accessible as they once were. Most people no longer farm, and fewer work as shepherds. Those metaphors, which resonated strongly with Jesus' followers, have lost some of their power. *Deeply Rooted* explores a powerful and accessible metaphor from *The Dialogue of Catherine of Siena*: the tree of your soul. Imagine a circle of good, rich soil on the ground. Picture a sprout coming from that rich soil that grows into a strong tree. Now imagine this tree branching out, blossoming, and bearing fruit. Your soul is like this tree. What you have imagined is part of Catherine's vision.

Who Was Catherine of Siena?

Caterina di Giacomo di Benincasa was born the twenty-third of twenty-five children in 1347 in Siena, Italy. When she was about six years old, she had an intense spiritual experience. While walking home with her brother, she happened to look across the Valle Piatta (Holy Child Valley) above the Church of the Preaching Friars. There she saw a vision of Christ seated on a throne, wearing a papal tiara with Peter, Paul, and John the Evangelist at his side. Christ extended his hand above Catherine, blessing her with the sign of the cross. Catherine became transfixed, unmoving and staring for a long time until her brother demanded her attention, and the vision was lost.[1] Catherine reportedly cut off her hair at the age of fifteen in response to feeling pressured to marry, an early example of the strength of her will. She joined the lay Dominican Order at eighteen.

By 1368, at the age of twenty-one, Catherine was working to serve the poor. She also began experiencing a series of intense mystical events, including one in 1370 in which she seemed lifeless to all observers for four hours. This event is sometimes referred to as her "mystical death." After establishing a monastery for women outside the city of Siena in 1377, Catherine experienced the visions that would eventually result in *The Dialogue*, which she referred to simply as "my book." As she worked on it, her health deteriorated quickly. In February 1380, she lost the use of her legs, and she eventually died on April 29, 1380.[2]

Catherine was canonized in 1461. Almost six hundred years later in 1939, she was named a patron saint of Italy, joining Saint Francis of Assisi. The influence of her writings continued to grow with time. In 1970, Pope Paul VI named her a Doctor of the Church.

The Metaphor

In an early section of *The Dialogue* titled "The Way of Perfection," God uses the image of a tree to explain to Catherine how various virtues work together in the Christian soul. The tree of the soul provides a powerful, timeless image because even today we understand how a tree grows—with dirt, seeds, water, roots, stem, sapling, and so on. The growth of our soul works in a similar way.

By exploring this metaphor, we will be able to create for ourselves a mental map to guide our spiritual growth as disciples of Jesus.

I have provided an English translation of the analogy in Appendix A. It is *not* easy reading; the text is complex. For example, the first sentence in the second paragraph is sixty-eight words long. After reading these two paragraphs many times, cross-referencing the ideas with other parts of *The Dialogue*, and reflecting on them for a long time, I think I can restate the metaphor in a way that might be a bit easier to understand.

Our souls are—or our spiritual growth is—like a tree. Imagine a circle on the ground. Within this space, the tree of our soul grows. The *width* of the circle is the knowledge of ourselves and the *depth* of the circle is our knowledge of God. With sufficient knowledge of self and God, the good soil of humility fills this space and the roots of love take hold. The tree grows strong when the soul exercises its powers of memory, understanding, and will, as well as three key virtues: patience, perseverance, and courage. The soul draws upon these traits for discernment, which leads to the tree's fruits: charity, prayer, and others.

That's it. Just seven sentences and 112 words. But these sentences are stuffed with meaning. With simple models, however, we face the danger of deceiving ourselves into believing we already fully understand a concept. We may understand the tenets of this metaphor intellectually—they make intuitive sense—but spiritual growth requires more than understanding. It requires practice and work—perhaps even a lifetime of both. I already know I will spend the rest of my life on earth pruning this tree, digging into the soil of humility. This book marks the beginning—not the end—of this journey, and I invite you to take it with me.

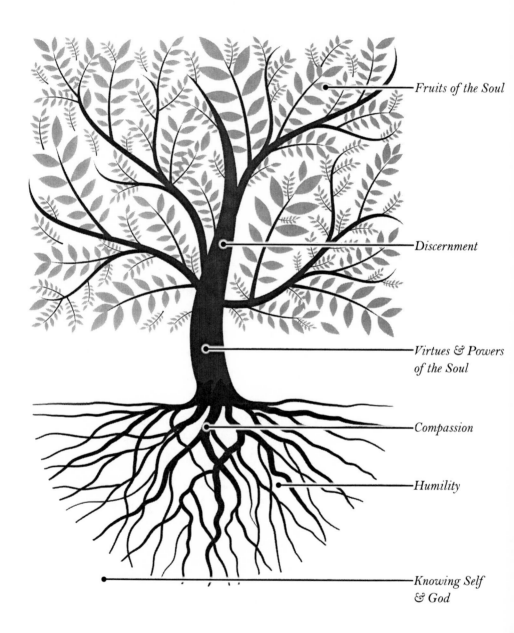

Fruits of the Soul

Discernment

Virtues & Powers of the Soul

Compassion

Humility

Knowing Self & God

THE TREE AT A GLANCE

The tree of the soul includes four major parts, and we will explore each part in two chapters. Each part concludes with a summary, prayer considerations, and suggestions for reflection. In each prayer consideration, I have suggested a connection to the Lord's Prayer, showing a way to reflect on the ideas from the chapter when reciting the prayer Jesus taught us. Prayer plays a critical role in spiritual growth, and I encourage readers to begin or conclude the work in each chapter with prayer.

A Note to Readers

As you move through the text, consider responding to reflection questions in writing. Putting pen to paper—or fingers to keyboard—can bring a new awareness of your thoughts and feelings. If you merely think about your learnings and questions without writing them down, you may forget them. With writing, you can review your thinking and check your perceptions at a later time.

Part I: The Garden

Chapter one begins with knowledge of self by focusing our awareness on our thoughts, feelings, and attachments. In chapter two, we reflect on our knowledge of God by considering God's goodness and mercy. In prayer, we focus on gaining awareness and insight into ourselves and reflect on the nature of God.

Part II: The Foundation

Chapter three demonstrates how knowledge of God and self leads us to the soil of humility, a core Christian virtue. In chapter four, we learn that the soil of humility is the foundation for the two great laws: love of God and love of neighbor. In prayer, we focus on our ego and how it can hinder our capacity for compassion.

Part III: Strength

Chapter five explores how the tree of our soul grows by exercising the soul's three unique powers: the gifts of memory, understanding, and will. Chapter six focuses on the three virtues of patience, persistence, and courage. In prayer, we reflect on and seek these gifts and the strength to love others as God loves us.

Part IV: Action

Chapter seven brings together what we have learned in the previous chapters into a process for discerning what action the soul should take. Chapter eight explores how we bring grace to others through four key fruits of our actions. We direct our prayer toward clarity of perception and the wisdom to choose actions that will glorify God.

Part V: Personal Practice

Spiritual growth requires change. God tells Catherine that the soul cannot stand still; instead, it moves either forward or backward.[1] So if we are not moving forward—not changing for the better—we might be backsliding. This section offers some guidance on how to integrate each aspect of the tree of the soul into a single reflective practice. Appendix A, as previously mentioned, includes translated text from *The Dialogue.* Appendix B offers suggestions for small-group facilitators.

PART I

THE GARDEN

I n the vision, God asks Catherine to imagine a garden and, within it, a circle inscribed upon the ground. In this circle, our souls begin to grow. This circle symbolizes the extent of our knowledge of ourselves and of God. Obviously, this circle ought to be a good size. A small circle would offer limited space— limited knowledge of ourselves and of God. As anyone who has ever tried to dig a hole for a fence post (or worse—replace a sprinkler head) knows, digging a deep hole in a narrow space proves difficult. When we dig a hole in the ground, we observe the relationship between the depth of the hole and the boundary of the circle in which we dig. If we had the choice of two circles inscribed on the ground—one just six inches wide and the other six feet wide—we would choose the wider circle to dig the deeper hole. Because of this fact, the first step in spiritual growth is to widen the circle—our knowledge of ourselves.

This starting point may confuse some. Why start with self? Shouldn't God be first? In our quest to better understand God, we may feel that we should purposefully avoid thinking about ourselves. We understand that we are not God. For that reason, we direct our searching and reflection toward heaven. God insists, however, that Catherine gain knowledge of herself because she cannot know the Almighty without knowing herself. God tells Catherine that if she wants to arrive at "perfect knowledge and enjoyment of Me, the Eternal Truth . . . never go outside the knowledge of yourself."[1] The knowledge of self and of God work together.

Spiritual growth requires gaining understanding about ourselves and God. As our knowledge of ourselves grows, our circle expands, giving us more space to dig deeper into our knowledge of God.

So what does it mean to "draw a circle"? The act of drawing a circle represents our spiritual practice; it represents the time and effort we devote to this work. If we do not dedicate time and effort to our spiritual lives, nothing will change. The diameter of the circle represents the time and effort we dedicate to understanding ourselves. This is the focus of chapter one. In chapter two, we'll focus on the depth of the circle—the time and effort we dedicate to increasing our knowledge of God. As we increase our knowledge of self and God, the circle expands, and the tree of our soul has room to grow. Let us now take a closer look at how we develop a greater awareness of self.

CHAPTER ONE

KNOWING SELF

We can liken the work of increasing our knowledge of ourselves to the work of a gardener. A gardener does not begin his or her work by tasting the fruit of the tree. Nor does the gardener work inside the tree, directing sap through its branches. Nor does the gardener make the trunk itself grow. The gardener does much of his or her initial work in the ground. So this image teaches us our first insight: Christian spiritual growth, like gardening, is a dirty bit of work. Not because of God—the Almighty is all good. But you and me? We are more complicated. True, we have parts that are quite good; but because we are human, we also have parts that are not so good. We have a dark side. While knowledge of God sounds delightful, knowledge of self may not be so.

Let's be completely candid. This kind of self-awareness can be difficult. Perhaps that's why Catherine, in a letter to a friend, used the phrase "the cell of true self-knowledge" in describing the mental discipline needed to know ourselves.[1] Looking within, confronting our best attributes alongside our darker character, can be lonely and challenging work. I've spent too many years looking up and looking around and not enough time looking within. We consider solitary confinement to be a harsh treatment; similarly, being left alone with our thoughts for long periods can bring out unexpected reflections and emotions. Fear not, however. As we will see in chapter six, patience is a premium virtue. We must be patient with ourselves as we begin one of the most difficult and rewarding tasks of Christian life: becoming more aware of ourselves.

How should we focus our attempts at self-knowledge? Philosophy, psychology, psychiatry, sociology, and even chemistry have provided a wealth of information about the human person. Our bodies contain sophisticated systems of bones, muscles, and internal organs. A complex mass of chemicals, neurons, and synapses make up our brains. But this type of knowledge is not where we begin. God tells Catherine that there are two aspects of the self: sensuality and reason. Our desires make up the aspect of sensuality. *The Dialogue* refers to sensuality often but never in a positive light. It refers to the selfish aspects of us that focus on pleasure—specifically, carnal pleasure. Sensuality must be tempered and controlled by the other aspect of the self: reason. Reason allows us to ask questions, reach understanding, and make judgments. It gives us the power to analyze our own thinking and behavior. Far be it from me to disagree with God, but I suggest the importance of distinguishing a third aspect of self that is related to but separate from thought and desire: feelings. Before exploring how sensuality, reason, and feelings can help us grow in self-knowledge, I offer a brief overview of how the three influence us.

God made our soul in God's image. God is love, and our soul needs to give and receive love to survive. That is its purpose. Jesus explains the uselessness of items that cannot fulfill their purpose. "You are the salt of the earth; but if salt has lost its taste, how can its saltiness be restored? It is no longer good for anything, but is thrown out and trampled under foot" (Matt. 5:13). The salt becomes worthless because it can no longer achieve the purpose for which it was created. A light is useless if a bushel prevents the light from shining. Just as an obstructed light cannot shine and the eye cannot see the light, an obstructed soul cannot love—cannot fulfill the purpose for which it was created.

What obstructs the soul? Feelings that distract us, thoughts that confuse us, and attachments that enslave us can obstruct the soul. We can increase our self-awareness by reflecting carefully on these three key aspects of self. Feelings often serve as a primary motivation for human behavior. Strong emotions can lead to quick action. Recognizing how our feelings affect us provides critical information on the path to self-awareness. The second obstruction is our thoughts. We can have thoughts (of which we may be totally unaware) that prevent us from perceiving the world clearly. Uncovering these thoughts increases self-awareness. The third obstruction is our attachments—the people, objects, or experience upon which we have come to depend for happiness. Our desire for them and fear of losing them can restrict our freedom. Let's look at each one more closely.

Feelings

Our emotions are powerful forces, and to understand ourselves, we need to understand how our feelings influence the way we perceive and react to everything around us. We'd like to think we are an intelligent and logical species—and we certainly can be— but there's a reason why the phrase "crimes of passion" exists. We often think and act based on our feelings. Therefore, we recognize the importance of increasing our awareness of our feelings.

Identifying how we feel can be difficult for some. It certainly was for me. In my late twenties, I saw a counselor once a week to help me both with the stress of work and a serious relationship.

One day, my counselor began with a simple question: "How are you feeling?" I spoke nonstop for at least ten minutes, recounting nearly every event in the previous seven days and how I had reacted to each one. She listened without interruption. When I finished, she said something like, "Thank you for telling me about your week and what you think about it. Now, how are you *feeling?*" I didn't know. I had to work hard to set aside thinking and consider my emotions.

Simple models for understanding emotions identify five to eight basic emotions. I have listed six below along with how those emotions may make us act and an image that depicts them. Some theorists reject the concept of basic emotions, but we needn't resolve that debate. We can simply become aware of the emotion we are experiencing. We don't have to get caught up in the nuances of emotional terms. Being *aware* of our experience is more important than *labeling* our experience.

Emotion	I experience . . .	Action
Fear	nervousness, anxiety, worry	Hiding
Anger	hostility, resentment	Fighting
Sadness	sorrow, grief, hurt	Crying
Peace	contentment	Relaxing
Affection	warmth for other people independent of desire	Hugging
Joy	happiness, excitement	Clapping

I did not include love in this list as I agree with many others that love—Christian love—is not a feeling. It is a verb. When Jesus says, "Love your neighbor," he isn't talking about how we ought to feel. He is telling us what to do. Jesus loves through action. He asks us to treat our neighbors with kindness, generosity, and consideration. We'll explore the concept of love more fully a bit later. The point here is that we may choose different basic terms to sort out our emotional experiences. However, our awareness must go beyond the identification of feelings to include six basic principles that can guide us in how we manage and respond to those feelings.

1. *Feelings are neither right nor wrong.* We needn't say to ourselves, "I shouldn't feel this way." We feel how we feel. Instead, we can work toward discovering what we feel and, if we can, why.

2. *Feelings are connected to experience.* Our feelings don't pop into our head without cause. They respond to experience. Something happens, and feelings arise in us in reaction to the experience.

3. *Feelings are connected to expectations.* We react emotionally to events in relation to our expectations for how our lives ought to be or what we want them to be. Identifying our expectation may be as easy as completing this statement: "I am having these feelings because I thought _____ was going to happen, not this."

4. *We can experience many different feelings at the same time.* We often become overwhelmed by a single feeling because of its intensity. But we will usually uncover more than one feeling if we take time to explore.

5. *Feelings vary in intensity.* To avoid letting the intensity of an emotional experience overwhelm us, we can ask ourselves the following two questions: (1) On a scale of 1–10, how powerful is the feeling? and (2) What past event that evoked this same feeling and level of intensity would help me understand the current feeling? Assigning a metric or a reference to our feelings can remind us that we have been able to work through similar feelings of that intensity before.

6. *Feelings are temporary.* Though feelings may vary in duration, they will come to an end. Our tears subside, our anger
   recedes, our exhilaration lessens, and our laughter fades.
   Because feelings are temporary, we need to exercise caution
   in reacting too quickly, especially when feelings are intense.
   A quick reaction may be appropriate in a dangerous situation,
   but if we are discerning a course of action that has moral or
   spiritual implications, we need to give ourselves more time
   for reflection. As scripture tells us, "A fool gives full vent to
   anger, but the wise quietly holds it back" (Prov. 29:11). The
   psychology of decision making reinforces this scriptural wisdom and emphasizes the importance of gaining emotional
   distance before making important decisions.

Whenever we feel agitated or stressed, we can remember
that emotions—like the tide—may crash against the shores of
our soul, but later they will retreat to the sea. If we offer ourselves the gift of time and thoughtful reflection, we may find it
easier to exercise the virtue of patience. I am reminded of something a resident in Pittsburgh, Pennsylvania, once told me about
the local weather. "If you don't like it, wait five minutes." In other
words, the rain will stop, the clouds will clear, and the sun will
shine. The conditions will change. In our spiritual journey, our
feelings do not provide a road map for determining direction.
Instead, they are our responses to the conditions through which
we travel.

Increasing Awareness of Feeling

We can improve our self-awareness of how we feel by
learning to ask and answer the following four questions.

1. What feelings am I experiencing?
2. How intense are these feelings?
3. How do these feelings influence my perception?
4. What do my feelings reveal to me about what I thought would have or should have happened?

Thoughts

Though much can be said—and has already been said—on the nature of thought, we will focus on how we can be aware of the kinds of thinking that will lead to self-knowledge as part of a spiritual discipline. We seek to be aware of the kind of thinking that deals with assumptions or biases. We define assumptions as ideas we have accepted as true without proof. A bias is usually expressed as unfair prejudice. Both can constrain our ability to correctly perceive the actions and events around us. As with feelings, sometimes thoughts can be outside our conscious awareness. We can uncover our thoughts by drawing attention to the labels we assign to people, actions, and beliefs.

When we see a homeless person with a cardboard sign asking for help, what is the first thought that comes to our mind? We may ask ourselves, *Is this person hungry? lazy? crazy? lying?* Notice how these adjectives—labels—carry unstated assumptions. The first (*hungry*) makes an assumption about the person's need. The second (*lazy*) makes an assumption about the person's work ethic. The third (*crazy*) makes an assumption about the person's mental capacity. The last (*lying*) reveals an assumption about the person's moral intent. We may believe any one of these labels; we may even believe all of them. But if the person is a stranger, we are using past experiences to prejudge the situation. We really don't know the stranger's need, work ethic, mental capacity, or intent. But making assumptions not based in fact offers us a way to judge a situation quickly. Sometimes a quick decision may seem necessary because we often don't have time to learn what we need to know in order to make an informed decision. We find it easier instead to use labels to justify decisions. But assumptions can be rationalizations for the intellectual laziness of avoiding the harder work of discernment.

Truths about Thoughts

1. *We may not be aware of all our thoughts.* Using the example above, we might have had an unpleasant past experience with a homeless person. Perhaps we have forgotten the experience, but the impact of it continues to shape our thinking about homeless people.

2. *Not all thoughts are worth sharing.* Our first thoughts are not always our best thoughts. The old adage my father taught me still has practical and spiritual value. Before speaking, we can ask ourselves the following: *Is it true? Is it kind? Is it necessary?*

3. *Not all thoughts are worth pursuing.* Our brain sometimes presents us with thoughts that come out of left field. We may ask ourselves, *Now where did* that *idea come from?* The thought may be funny or unkind. It also could be a hostile thought or one that invites violence. If thoughts truly result from electrochemical activity in our brain, we may not be responsible for thoughts that occur to us unbidden. But for most of us, we *are* responsible for the thoughts we choose to pursue.

4. *We don't have to give unexpected thoughts attention.* When family or friends call and we don't feel up to a conversation, we let the call go to voice mail. A student raising his hand in school does not guarantee that the teacher will call upon him. Just

because someone knocks does not obligate us to open the door. Unexpected thoughts have no claim on us; we are free to decline them.

As soon as we recognize an unwelcome thought, we can try to limit our exposure to it. One therapist suggested the following: Look up, count to three, and pick a favorite memory to replace the unwelcome thought. She even recommended keeping our top ten memories on an index card. I think funny ones work best.

Whether we share our thoughts or pursue them, our goal is to be aware of our thoughts. By bringing our thoughts into awareness, we can account for how those thoughts influence us.

The Forgotten Thought

After many years, I recognized my own bias about hair. Yes, *hair.* Some years ago, my brother decided to shave his head. He said it would be easier to keep clean. His newly shaved head required less maintenance, and he didn't want the hassle of managing longer hair. The first time I saw him, I was caught off guard. I did not like it; I thought it made him look mean. My thought shaped how I perceived his behavior. I felt he was severe, more intense, and, honestly, a little cold. Only this year—more than a decade later—I began to understand my reaction.

Twenty years ago, a man with a shaved head murdered a friend of a friend. That was the image I held of men with shaved heads. I was stunned to recognize that it still affected me. To deal with this thought, I intentionally chose a new image. My brother does not look like that person. He looks like Patrick Stewart, the actor, who has often played intelligent and compassionate characters. My brother has not changed his appearance, but he looks different to me now. Becoming aware of my thinking changed my experience.

Increasing Awareness of Thoughts

To increase our awareness of what we think, we can ask ourselves the following three questions:

1. What similar past experience influences how I perceive what I see and hear?
2. How am I labeling the actions, statements, or appearance of others?
3. What attitudes, behaviors, or intent do I associate with the labels?

Attachments

In *The Dialogue,* God does not define the word *sensuality,* but almost every time God uses it, the term describes something we ought to avoid. I would define *sensuality* as "a dedication to or preoccupation with bodily pleasures and overindulging in carnal desires." Sensual pleasures needn't be sinful or evil, but when we love the things of this world too much, when we chase them and leave our desire for God behind, we are in danger of loving things inordinately—at a level or intensity that is not good for our soul. This may have been what God meant when God tells Catherine that "the delights of this world, without Me, are venomous thorns."[2]

While carnal desire seems to be the focus of God's message, sensuality is just one kind of desire. We have all kinds of desires, and any of them in excess can be dangerous. Broadly, we have desires for acquisition (wealth, property, political power), recognition (fame, popularity, success), and stimulation (eating, drinking, smoking, drugs, sex, video games, or social media). In moderation, most of these are not evil. We don't condemn eating, blogging, or running for political office. But when taken to extremes, these pursuits can ruin us.

An attachment is a desire to which we have given more attention, importance, or energy than is appropriate. God explains that attachments move the soul by so preoccupying our mind and heart that there is little room left for God.[3] We have filled our mind and heart with our attachments to worldly things. We have to let our attachments go. Once we have emptied our heart of attachments to worldly things, God can fill it with divine love and grace. I believe this is what Jesus tells us in Matthew 6:21: "Where your treasure is, there your heart will be also." God wants us to guard our affections and not give them away lightly. Furthermore, the writer of the book of James explains that "one is tempted by one's own desire, being lured and enticed by it; then, when that desire has conceived, it gives birth to sin" (1:14-15). We need to study these desires that are independent of or in conflict with our desire for God and our efforts to satisfy them. These desires separate us from God.

In *The Rhythm of Being: The Unbroken Trinity,* Raimon Pannikar suggests that "desire is the opposite of freedom."[4] When we want things, our freedom to choose is compromised. The desire tugs at us and creates a spiritual conflict of interest— I want something not of God, but I also want God. Spiritual freedom comes from shedding desires that are not part of the will of God. We may not be able to relinquish our desires, but through self-knowledge, we can learn to see past them and reach the point where our attachments no longer distort our ability to perceive clearly.[5]

As with feelings and thoughts, self-awareness challenges us to do more than identify our attachments. We need to be guided by what we know and believe about the nature of attachments.

Truths about Attachments

1. *All humans have attachments.* It is not possible to force yourself to stop wanting something that you want.
2. *Attachments are the opposite of freedom.* Attachments restrict us by capturing our attention and influencing our actions.
3. *Pursuing attachments is a choice.* We can unconsciously choose to pursue an attachment, but we can only make the choice not to pursue it when we recognize the attachment exists.

Increasing Awareness of Attachments

In order to grow in our ability to identify our attachments, we can ask ourselves the following questions:

1. To which of my belongings have I attached too much importance? (Or what new possession has caught my attention?)
2. In what ways am I seeking the validation or recognition I think I need to be happy?
3. Which activities or interests are taking more of my time than they should, possibly causing me to neglect other important tasks?

Awareness, Not Rejection

We have been exploring what it means to know ourselves as a first step toward spiritual practice. The goal of this self-reflection is to broaden the breadth of our self-understanding (create a wider circle) so that we create enough spiritual space to deepen our understanding of God (dig a deeper hole). This self-knowledge includes emotions (what we feel), reason (what we think), and attachments (what we want). Increasing our awareness does not mean we overcome or remove these forces; we simply recognize them. Our goal cannot be to rid ourselves of feelings, thoughts, and attachments. Instead we choose to be conscious and mindful of what triggers them and how they affect us.

We have all heard the saying, "Keep your friends close and your enemies closer." So it is with our thoughts, feelings, and attachments. We should know them and stay aware of them, but we cannot let them define us. Consider the difference between saying, "I am having a sad feeling" and "I *am* sad." Recognizing our current emotional experience is healthy, but we are not our emotions. We are much more than those. We are not our thoughts or desires; we are more than those as well. We strive toward a way of life that does not allow thoughts, feelings, and desires to consume us. We will know ourselves better when we can identify our thoughts, feelings, and desires and take them into account as we react to the world around us.

The Road Trip of Life

Life is a road trip. The actions we take in life are like driving an automobile. Our soul drives the car. The destination—grace. Attachment constantly tells us what it wants. Emotion yells about the destination and the route. Thinking tries to read the directions and look for landmarks. None of them has all the answers, and finding our way can be very confusing. Sometimes we want to eject one of the passengers from the car. But we can't—they come with the car. They are part of human existence. We all have them—all the time. As we grow in self-awareness, we learn to recognize and consider our thoughts, feelings, and attachments—taking everything into account—to choose the most appropriate course.

Our thoughts, feelings, and attachments can dramatically influence our behavior if we are unaware of them. Awareness exposes these forces and makes them visible to our soul. Their power over us is lessened when we understand them, and we move closer to freedom. In this freedom, we may choose to act in accordance with our thoughts, feelings, and attachments, or we may defy them. Either way, our decision constitutes a real choice. Real freedom of choice—an exercise of our own will— can only be achieved with an awareness of ourselves. This freedom includes the ability to choose to love God. If we are not aware of our thoughts, feelings, and attachments, we may not be truly free. If we are not free, we cannot fully love others or God. The wisdom God imparts to Catherine now makes sense. "If you will arrive at a perfect knowledge and enjoyment of Me . . . you should never go outside the knowledge of yourself."[6]

As we work toward increasing our self-knowledge, we will be observers and not judges. We are not judging ourselves— that's God's job. Instead, we will practice identifying our thoughts, feelings, and attachments. The journey of growing in self-awareness may exhaust us, but we remind ourselves of this good news: Awareness can be one of the biggest tools in our spiritual toolbox. It is bigger than our thoughts, bigger than our feelings, bigger even than our desires. Our awareness ranks above all of these. Awareness sits in the corner of our being and watches the feeler, observes the thinker, and studies the desirer. Awareness—the ability to observe all three—is a powerful tool for spiritual growth.

Summary

- Knowing ourselves is the first step toward knowing God.
- Self-knowledge means increasing our awareness of our feelings, thoughts, and attachments.

- Feelings are neither right nor wrong.
- Feelings are connected to our experiences and expectations.
- We can have many feelings at the same time.
- Feelings vary in intensity and duration.
- We may not be aware of all our thoughts.
- Not all thoughts are worth sharing.
- We can choose whether to pursue a particular thought or attachment.
- All humans have attachments.
- Attachments are the opposite of freedom.
- Our goal is to identify our feelings, thoughts, and attachments without placing judgment on ourselves.

Prayer

A common translation of the Lord's Prayer contains the following line: "And lead us not into temptation, but deliver us from evil." My wife once told me that the Spanish version could be translated as "Let us not fall into temptation," and I now prefer this language. I do not believe God ever leads me toward anything bad. I may fall into temptation, but usually I have engineered my own fall through an unhealthy desire for something unconnected to my desire for God. When I say the words *Let us not fall into temptation,* I focus on a single idea: freedom from desires. I pray for the strength to stop pursuing or clinging to attachments that interfere with my path to God.

As you attempt to increase your self-awareness, direct your prayer toward insight. Begin with a simple request:

Lord, give me the grace to understand my thoughts, feelings, and desires. Amen.

Then look to Psalm 139.

O LORD, you have searched me and known me.
You know when I sit down and when I rise up;
    you discern my thoughts from far away.
You search out my path and my lying down,
    and are acquainted with all my ways.
Even before a word is on my tongue,
    O LORD, you know it completely. . . .
Search me, O God, and know my heart;
    test me and know my thoughts.

(vv. 1-4, 23)

For Reflection

Identify your feelings about a certain event without expressing
those feelings. For example, tell yourself, *I am feeling a little angry
right now*, instead of yelling or being aggressive.

Identify your attitudes or biases in the situation by examin-
ing the labels you have applied to others. What are the judgments behind your labels?

Be honest with yourself about the outcome you want in the
situation. Ask yourself, *What's in it for me? If I didn't care about
anyone else, what would I do?* By doing this, you will reveal those
desires of which you may be unaware.

CHAPTER TWO

KNOWING GOD

Having expanded the circle of knowledge of self, we now turn our attention to our circle's depth. We are going to dig down, focusing on our knowledge of God. How shall we even begin to know God better? The challenge seems daunting. We need a starting point that gives us some guidance as well as confidence. Over the centuries, some theologians and Christian mystics have suggested four premises that help us begin this journey.

God is transcendent. The Divine Mystery is beyond limited human thinking. We are incapable of knowing God fully. We approach the Divine Mystery with the admission that we are never going to fully understand God—at least not while we are on earth. So we must begin with intellectual humility. God is more than we can conceive. Christian mystics spoke about the Cloud of Unknowing. They agreed that we begin a journey toward knowing God by admitting that we know that we do not know.

God is beyond our vocabulary. Because God is beyond full understanding, we do not have much to say about God. No words can fully describe God. No right combination of words in the right sequence will reveal the mystery of the Creator. So we begin our journey in silence. We have to get beyond words—even beyond our unspoken thoughts—in order to reach a space where our spirit can be still.

So far, the journey toward knowing God sounds pretty difficult. Our words are inadequate and our minds are not up to the task. The good news is that two other foundational premises soften this ground.

We are more than mind and body. This premise proclaims that our human understanding is not limited to the senses and the mind. Human understanding has three aspects. The first is that which we perceive by our senses. God invites Catherine to "rise above your senses so that you may more surely know the truth."[1] The second aspect of human understanding is that which is disclosed to our minds. The third is that which is revealed to our spirit. Some call this third aspect of human understanding mystical insight, some the "third eye" or the eye of faith. We are capable, as children of God, of "seeing" in this other way so we need to exercise and cultivate our ability.

Jesus reinforces this idea when answering the question, What is the greatest commandment? Jesus says, "You shall love the Lord your God with all your heart, and with all your soul, and with all your mind, and with all your strength" (Mark 12:30). In other words, we love God with every part of ourselves—with our senses, with our mind, and with our spirit. We can assume this aspect of human awareness, this "other way of knowing," is accessible to us because Jesus instructs us to know God with our entire being.

Jesus commands us to love (know) God with all that we are, and we are more than mind and body. We can move toward God with the confidence that we are capable of this divine insight. We may call this insight *faith*—an openness to the Divine Mystery that is beyond the senses and the mind but not beyond our spirit.

We trust this kind of awareness is available to us and that we can reach it. It is possible for us to move past the threshold of what we see and understand and gaze into that which is hidden and only accessible by our spirit.

A good example of divine insight is a rainbow. Just recently I was driving with my children, Sarah and Nicholas, on a rainy winter day, and we saw a rainbow to the east. We talked about how rainbows are made, and one of them was reminding me how the water refracts the sunlight and reveals the different colors. As we talked about it further, we reached this revelation: The entire spectrum of color is always present in the light all around us. Rain doesn't *create* rainbows; rain *reveals* the colors that are already present in the atmosphere. This color spectrum is usually hidden from our sight and only revealed under special conditions. In the same way, we may have moments of insight and revelation that reveal to us—or at least suggest to us—the presence of the Divine that is often hidden but no less real.

God is with us. The premise, which is perhaps the most encouraging, maintains God's immanence, meaning God is within us. Indeed, as scripture tells us, "[God] is not far from each one of us" (Acts 17:27). The spirit of God is near and accessible to us. The writer of Revelation tells us, "See, the home of God is among mortals. He will dwell with them; they will be his peoples, and God himself will be with them" (21:3).

We can understand why God tells Catherine that she must never leave her cell of self-knowledge in order to know God. When we dwell deep within ourselves, we connect with the holiness within us. Our belief in the nearness of God provides one definition for *hope*. As Raimon Panniker reminds us, "hope is not of the future. Hope should not be confused with a certain optimism about the future which only betrays a pessimism of the present"[2] Instead, hope is a revelation in the present moment that suggests the possibility that there is more to reality than what our senses perceive or our minds comprehend.

The four premises that guide us on our journey toward gaining knowledge of God can be boiled down to four words: (1) *humility*—because we cannot fully know God, (2) *silence*—because our words are not sufficient to describe God, (3) *faith*—because we are capable of understanding beyond our senses and our mind, and (4) *hope*—because we are created in the image of the Divine.

With these foundational words in place, we enter into the task of trying to know God. What is it we should know about God? Jesus tells us that "no one knows the Father except the Son and anyone to whom the Son chooses to reveal him" (Matt. 11:27). In other words, we best begin with what God has disclosed to us. Throughout *The Dialogue*, God consistently refers to two overarching attributes to describe the Divine nature. These attributes reinforce what scripture tell us about God.

First, God is good. God assures Catherine of God's supreme and inexhaustible goodness. Both the Old and New Testaments speak at length about God's goodness. I offer the four following examples: "O give thanks to the LORD, for he is good; for his steadfast love endures forever" (Ps. 107:1); "If you then, who are evil, know how to give good gifts to your children, how much more will your Father in heaven give good things to those who ask him!" (Matt. 7:11); "For everything created by God is good" (1 Tim. 4:4); and "Every generous act of giving, with every perfect gift, is from above" (James 1:17).

Second, God is merciful. "My mercy is without any comparison, far more than you can see."[3] The New Testament encourages us to trust in this mercy. "Let us therefore approach the throne of grace with boldness, so that we may receive mercy and find grace to help in time of need" (Heb. 4:16). In the Gospels, Jesus proclaims and demonstrates mercy by extending forgiveness to those who have sinned. (See John 8:3-11; Luke 7:36-50; Luke 23:39-43; Luke 15:11-32.)

How to Know God Better

In *The Dialogue*, Catherine does not record specific instructions on how to know God. But I have found that my own connection with God flows from six primary sources that coincide with God's message to Catherine.

1. *The Word*. Scripture is a faith treasure. Both the Hebrew scriptures and the New Testament offer great insight into the nature of God. In the Gospels, we understand God through the actions and words of Jesus. In *The Dialogue*, God uses the phrase "My Truth" to refer to God's wisdom. But God also uses the very same phrase to refer to Jesus, often in tandem with the phrase "Word Incarnate." God makes it clear that the nature of the Almighty is revealed in Jesus, affirming that Jesus speaks the truth when he says, "The Father is in me and I am in the Father" (John 10:38). By ensuring that God's Word is a part of our lives, we grow closer to God. We may prefer to spend a few minutes every day with the Bible or more time just once a week. Either way, making the Word of God a regular part of our lives is important. This time can also include learning more about the scriptures by taking classes, participating in study groups, and reading the work of other great Christian authors.

2. *Prayer.* Spending time in prayer is essential to knowing God. As we will see later, prayer is one of the fundamental fruits of the tree of the soul, especially intercessory prayer. God tells Catherine that there is no other way to taste the truth than "by means of humble and continuous prayer."[+] God offers prayer as the process for revelation. In prayer, we humble ourselves before the Lord and sing God's glory.

3. *Creation.* Extraordinary natural beauty covers the earth. Immersing myself in God's creation always fills me with delight and wonder. My kids are very accustomed to me running inside the house and saying, "Hey! The sunset is awesome. Hurry outside!" They never hesitate. They get up, run outside, and stare with me at the sky, noting the changing colors, the cloud formations, and the descending sun. Nature has played an important part of my family vacations. My children and I love going to the mountains or the ocean and finding joy and serenity in the world God has given us.

   In the summer of 2013, my wife and I visited Mendocino, California. We stood under an arched trellis in front of a small inn. A hummingbird of exquisite color zoomed by and hovered at a bush less than a foot away. The hummingbird was not in a hurry, so this moment lasted for at least a full minute, possibly longer. My wife and I became statues. We stared at the bright color of the hummingbird's chest, the ceaseless blur of her wings, and the precision with which she approached each flower. If there was any sound, I don't recall it. Even though my senses perceived and my mind understood what was happening before me, I was no less in awe of the hummingbird. That any animal could move its wings that fast while remaining still seemed incredible to me. The hummingbird offered a beautiful glimpse of the glory of creation.

4. *Gifts.* We all possess talents. They come in many forms and combinations. When we appreciate and celebrate these gifts, we come a bit closer to God, the source of all gifts. Some of us play music or dance. Some write, draw, paint, sculpt, or take photographs. Some are skilled scientists while others possess a knack for comedy. Through the Internet and social media, people can share and express their talents globally, bringing them spiritual insight, compassion, laughter, and inspiration. Our gifts can offer grace to us; they are signs of God's spirit moving within us and among us.

   For example, the innocence and affection of young children is a gift we can all appreciate. When we look past the noise, chaos, and distraction of children, we see their capacity for being open and loving—and this can bring us closer to God. The hug of a child holds power because it models the affection and trust that we are told to show God. The gift of parental love—a love that strives to be unconditional and limitless even in our imperfection—helps us understand God's love.

5. *Community.* Jesus creates a community of disciples, and they journey together with Jesus for years while learning about God. Jesus uses this model to teach us. When I am disconnected from a community of faith, my own personal faith development slows down. Through my own experience, I have found two overarching characteristics of faith communities that help me grow closer to God. First, the worship of the community must be vibrant, and, for me, music is central to that purpose. In fact, I'm not sure I would know how to worship God without music. Second, the community has to feel warm and inviting. My worship community needs to be

a place where I feel welcomed and encouraged to meet and form relationships with others.

6. *Service.* Jesus's life is marked by his service. Jesus tells us how to proclaim the kingdom; he asks that we be a source of healing and forgiveness for others. We can see the value of service through psychological research regarding happiness. People who volunteer report that they are happier than people who do not. When we serve others, we rise above our own problems and recognize that others around us are also suffering or in need of companionship and connection. God told Catherine that when we deprive our neighbor of charity, harm is done not only to our neighbor but also to ourselves because we deprive ourselves of the grace that comes from giving. By serving others, we create space in our heart for the grace of God.

God expresses goodness and mercy through relationship. When we read the Bible or meet God in prayer, we examine our relationship with God. In nature, we celebrate our relationship with God's creation. Through our gifts, our community, and our service toward others, we explore our relationship with our neighbor. God is all around us. We just need to look. "When you search for me, you will find me; if you seek me with all your heart" (Jer. 29:13).

Our efforts to increase our knowledge of God play a critical role in the health of our soul. Our spiritual practice must include consciously reflecting on the nature of the Divine, which God has disclosed to us through Jesus, the prophets, and scripture. God suggests that our spiritual practice will lead us to one of the core virtues of Christian living—humility—which is the focus of chapter three.

Summary

- We approach knowing God with a grounding in four beliefs.

  - God is transcendent. We cannot fully know the Divine because that knowledge is beyond human understanding.
  - God is beyond our vocabulary. We may find ourselves keeping silence because our words for God are not sufficient.
  - We are more than mind and body. We believe in God's promise that we can know the Divine with our mind, body, and spirit.
  - God is with us. We believe in God's immanence because we are made in the image and likeness of God.

- We can know God better through scripture, prayer, creation, gifts, community, and service.

Prayer

For many, the search for God lies at the heart of prayer. Prayer becomes an appeal for revelation, that God's goodness and mercy will somehow be made known through a desire to know the Creator. This desire was articulated succinctly by Moses: "Show me your glory, I pray" (Exod. 33:18).

The Lord's Prayer contains two sections that help you reflect on and pray for a greater knowledge of God. The first line of the prayer, "Our Father, who art in heaven, hallowed be thy name," reminds you that you should enter into the presence of God with great reverence for the Almighty and personal humility in that holy presence. Later in the prayer, the line "Give us this day our daily bread," reminds you of your reliance on God's goodness. This triggers a sentiment of gratitude and leads you back to the humility that comes from admitting your absolute dependence on God. Using the Lord's Prayer or the prayer below, you can speak with God.

> *Holy God, you encompass more than my senses and mind can comprehend. I know that I do not know, and all my words are not enough. But I have faith in your commandment to love you with all my senses, all my mind, and all my soul. I believe that I am created in your image, and this gives me hope that you are near. Open my spirit to your goodness and mercy. Amen.*

For Reflection

If God is beyond your thoughts and words, how does this affect your prayer life? If God is immanent, how does that change how you treat yourself and others? How are you seeking God with all your heart? Where are you looking for God?

PART II

THE FOUNDATION

I n Part I, we focused on expanding our circle, increasing its
width by becoming more aware of ourselves and increasing its
depth by reflecting on our knowledge of God. Part I encouraged
us to create a good space in which our tree—our soul—can grow
strong. As with real trees, the tree of our soul requires two basic
initial ingredients that are essential for its future: good soil and
strong roots. However, we cannot grow strong roots without
soil. Soil comes first.

What is good soil for the soul? With what do we fill this
hole we've created? Generally, good soil is made up of about 25
percent water and 25 percent air (made mostly of oxygen and
nitrogen). The other half is made of stone, clay, and organic matter—decaying plant and animal life. We are not surprised to
learn that soil is half air and water—things we know we need in
order to live as much as trees do. But what is the spiritual equiva-
lent of good dirt? Answer: *humility*. Just as trees wither and die

without good soil, our soul will not grow without humility. With that soil in place, roots can form in the earth, and as they grow deep and strong, the tree moves out of the ground and toward the light. Chapter three will focus on the soil of humility. We'll look at the roots of our soul in chapter four.

CHAPTER THREE

HUMILITY

God suggests to Catherine that humility is the appropriate response to knowledge of God and self. When we contemplate God's goodness, we see immediately that all good things are a gift from above. When we reflect on the mercy of God, we can more easily stop judging others and start helping them. When I admit that the wisdom of God is much greater than what I know, I embrace humility.

Humility is one of the most powerful principles that God impresses upon Catherine. While charity remains the queen of the virtues (as we'll see later), God points to humility as "the foster-mother and nurse of charity."[1] The soil of humility is "that which gives life to the tree, to its branches, and its root."[2] Our tree of the soul must be grounded in humility. God's explanation tells us how important humility is, but it does not tell us *what* humility is. What is humility? Sometimes, when we cannot define a word, we first define its opposite. God does the same for Catherine by describing the opposite of humility: pride.

The chief human vice is self-love, and it expresses itself primarily through pride. God calls pride "the enemy of humility and charity."[3] We see pride in a number of behaviors. Pride begins with love of our own reputation.[4] This creates a soul full of pride that fails to praise God. Instead, God explains, the proud soul "robs Me of the honor due to Me, and attributes it to herself, through vainglory."[5]

We extend this contempt to our neighbor by being judgmental, which leads us to believe we are better than others. We see this play out in several ways. For example, we may be scandalized by our neighbor, which leads to a judgmental thought that places us above our neighbor. It sounds like this: "I can't believe that the people next door. . . ." A second indicator of pride is being offended—*How dare you!* we might think. These thoughts encourage us to feel slighted and feed our pride.

When we think we are better than others, we can become impatient, acting poorly when what we think we deserve is delayed or denied and punishing our neighbors by treating them discourteously. This impatience becomes the justification for disobedience.[6] *It's okay for me to break the rules,* we tell ourselves, *because I am better and I shouldn't have to wait.* God warns Catherine that when souls have "drawn their nourishment" from the roots of pride instead of humility, the result is ingratitude.[7] In other words, when we are rooted in pride rather than humility, we may come to believe we have earned, and therefore deserve, all that we have. We eventually become ungrateful. A lack of humility causes real consequences. Self-love, impatience, disobedience, and ingratitude lead to a lack of discernment and poor decisions.

God identifies the following signs of pride for Catherine: being judgmental of our neighbor, showing impatience, acting ungrateful, and lacking in praise for God. The opposites of these reveal the characteristics of humility.

Being nonjudgmental is the first aspect of humility. Are we aware of the critical adjectives we attach to others in our thoughts? To counter this habit, we can replace the labels with *child of God*. We can try this method with people who tend to frustrate us or with strangers in public by observing what words come to mind when we watch others. Then we choose to give up those words. When we admit to ourselves that we really don't know the souls of others, we can ask ourselves, *What do they need?* or *What is their deepest hurt?*

Patience is the second aspect of humility, and we define it as having a great attitude while enduring delay, frustration, or suffering. What attitude are we displaying for others when we are forced to wait? We'll discuss patience more fully in chapter six because God names patience as one of three premium virtues.

Gratitude marks the third dimension of humility. We demonstrate gratitude when showing appreciation to others for their kindness, no matter how small, or in prayer when we thank God for the blessings of the day. Gratitude means offering thanks for every assistance from strangers, no matter how insignificant. We know we have received blessings in our lives. So let's count them. Literally. We can make a list of things, people, and situations for which we are grateful.

Praise for God is the fourth dimension of humility. We can express our praise for God in limitless ways. Four common ways to offer praise are delighting in the beauty of God's creation, reading scripture, dancing, and singing. We don't have to be musicians to use music as a form of praise. For those who don't feel comfortable singing, they can sit and breathe and let the music of praise fill their heart and mind. Another option would be to read the psalms that praise God.

In my own prayer life, I focus on four aspects of praising God that resonate with me personally. I praise God for being eternal, holy, and the Creator. The fourth element of praise is joy. I combined verses from Psalms 90; 98; 103; and 148 into a short prayer of praise: *O Lord, from everlasting to everlasting you are God and all that is within me blesses your holy name. Praise God, sun and moon; praise the Lord, all you shining stars. With trumpets and the sound of the horn, make a joyful noise before the Almighty.*

I usually use this prayer at the beginning of the day, but I also could use it whenever I enter into prayer.

Humility in Scripture

God's instruction on humility is consistent with the teachings of Jesus, who makes it clear that we ought to humble ourselves before God and others. He praises the prayer of the tax collector—"God, be merciful to me, a sinner!" (Luke 18:13). While dining with some Pharisees, Jesus tells them the parable of the wedding guest to illustrate how the proud seek recognition and status. (See Luke 14:7-11.) The Pharisees want to be noticed, like those who pray aloud on the street corners. (See Matthew 6:5.) Instead, Jesus praises those who are patient enough to serve others, which is one of the lessons of his parable of the good Samaritan. (See Luke 10:25-37.) Jesus also tells his disciples more than once that he expects humility as they follow him. He says, "You know that the rulers of the Gentiles lord it over them, and their great ones are tyrants over them. It will not be so among you; but whoever wishes to be great among you must be your servant, and whoever wishes to be first among you must be your slave" (Matt. 20:25-27).

A Gospel Story on Humility

Jesus' story of the laborers in the vineyard illustrates humility and connects it to the practice of knowing ourselves. (See Matthew 20:1-16.) In the story, the landowner pays the workers who arrived last a full day's wage—the same as those workers who began early in the day. This causes some anger among workers who worked a full day. Why are they angry? Why can they not praise God for the boon given to their fellows? Why can't they be happy for the good fortune of the workers who come late? Why can't they say, "Wow, you got a full day's wage? You are lucky! That is so great. I'm glad for you." To be honest, I'm not sure I would have said those things either.

Applying the principle of knowing ourselves to the full-day workers may help us understand their reaction. First, what are they thinking? What labels have they applied to the workers who come late to the vineyard? Perhaps they assume the late workers are lazy. Second, what are the full-day workers feeling? Probably a touch of envy because the workers who came late are getting the better deal, which understandably leads to anger and resentment. If someone offered me the same amount of money for less work, I'm pretty sure I would take it. Desire, of course, compounds all of this. What do the all-day workers want? They want more money, and their argument makes sense to many of us. They want to be treated equitably, to be paid on a pro rata basis. In other words, more work equals more money.

These full-day laborers are blinded by their judgments and the adjectives they have applied to the late workers. Their emotional reaction of anger also obscures their perception. Their desire for more leads them to perceive an act of generosity to others as a personal slight to themselves. The vineyard owner challenges the full-day workers who are complaining: "Am I not allowed to do what I choose with what belongs to me? Or are you envious because I am generous?" (Matt. 20:15). The full-day workers cannot see the landowner's act as generous because they are biased by their judgments, emotions, and desires. If they were humble, they could praise God for the landowner's generosity, be truly grateful for someone else's good fortune, and have a pleasant attitude about the experience.

Humility and Experience

We sometimes misunderstand humility. Humility is not self-deprecating; it does not ask us to pretend that we do not have gifts. It also does not mean that we deny ourselves simply to exercise asceticism. Yes, Jesus teaches us to take the lowest seat at the wedding banquet and not to presume the place of honor. Humility includes this principle, but humility is more than that. To embrace humility, we have to get past two bad habits: believing that others are responsible for our experience—that others impose our feelings, thoughts, and desires upon us—and assuming that our experience is objectively true.

As we achieve more clarity about what's going on inside us, we can begin to take the next step—admitting that our experience is coming from within us. Let's use a simple example. Many of us work with difficult people. Put bluntly, these people make us crazy. Imagine my reaction when a colleague suggested to me that the negative feelings I encounter when interacting with these people can only be blamed on me. "Wait," I said. "You mean it's *my* fault? You are kidding me!" But he wasn't kidding. Those feelings were coming from me and from no one else. Even if several people agree that a certain person is hard to get along with, that only proves that several people have similar expectations for how that person should behave and he or she consistently fails those standards. Truthfully, anger and frustration are the result of expectations we have for others' behavior (or for outcomes we are hoping for) and the importance we attach to them. They are coming from inside us. That does not mean we should not give appropriate feedback or correction. But our internal experience belongs to us alone. So what if we admit we are the source of our own experience? Well, that brings us to the second point—the assumption that our version of reality is completely accurate.

Everyone has an internal experience, feelings, and emotions that are all his or her own. Our internal experience is not more important than others' experiences and may not reflect what's really going on. Our own version of an event may not be the whole story. Recognizing this requires humility. When I blow my stack because of an annoying colleague, I am punishing that person (and everyone else who must listen to my rant) for the expectations I have of his or her behavior and the importance I attach to them. I am also presuming that my experience is more accurate than anyone else's experience. But it isn't.

Humility is about setting aside the self—overcoming our natural tendency to assume our perceptions are reality. Just as we cannot fully understand God with our limited understanding and inadequate vocabulary, we also may not fully understand what's happening around us. Admitting that our experience is not the sum total of reality creates space for us to focus more on the experiences of others, reflecting with compassion on what they need. Once we recognize our internal thoughts, feelings, and desires, we can learn from them. They can inform our actions when they are helpful, or we can prevent them from driving our interactions with others when they're not helpful.

Once we understand that we are creating our own experience—when we accept the truth of that—we can move forward in two ways. First, we can create a different experience for ourselves by adjusting our expectations. Second, we can open our mind to the experience others are having and strive for greater understanding of how they perceive events.

Summary

- Humility is the appropriate response to our own thoughts, feelings, and desires and to God's wisdom, mercy, and goodness.
- Humility encompasses four actions: being nonjudgmental, showing patience, acting grateful, and praising God.
- Humility admits that our experience is no more important than anyone else's and may not be accurate.

Prayer

In prayer, you praise God for all the good that you see around you, regardless of your role in it. The Lord's Prayer begins with humility. "Our Father, who art in heaven, hallowed be thy name" is a clear admission of reverence for the Almighty. Jesus teaches you to enter into prayer by recognizing the greatness of your God, and this naturally moves your mind and heart to a humbler posture. "Give us this day our daily bread" reminds you to be grateful for all you have. "Forgive us our trespasses, as we forgive those who trespass against us" helps you avoid being judgmental about your neighbor.

Your prayer might be as simple as, "Lord, I am not worthy to have you come under my roof" (Matt. 8:8).

For Reflection

In what ways are you praising God regularly? judging others? demonstrating gratitude to God and others for the good you have received? discounting the experience of others? assuming your perceptions are completely accurate?

CHAPTER FOUR

COMPASSION

The brilliant metaphor God provides Catherine explains that soil sustains the tree of the soul. The tree absolutely depends upon the soil—not only for growth but also for its very life. Deepening humility is the core spiritual practice for disciples of Jesus. Humility must be cultivated so that the soul can grow strong. All our exploration, all our awareness—of ourselves and of God—will come to naught if it does not lead us to humility. Properly tilled and constantly fertilized through awareness, this now-rich soil of humility fills the circle of your awareness, allowing roots to grow. The roots that grow in this humble soil also have a name—*love.*

God reminds Catherine of the promise of Jesus: "For where two or three are gathered in my name, I am there among them" (Matt. 18:20). Those of us familiar with the Gospels and with Jesus' famous words have usually been taught that the "two or three" refer to persons. This makes sense because in Matthew this verse follows an explanation by Jesus for how to deal with members of the faith community who have strayed from the path. Jesus encourages us to confront them alone (to correct them in private as not to embarrass them). If unsuccessful, we are to bring one or two witnesses. If two cannot convince the accused, Jesus encourages us to take the problem to the church. His reasoning, of course, is that when we gather together as a Christian community, we are better able to address conflict, arrive at the spirit of truth, and act in accordance with God's will for us. That is still good advice.

But God offers Catherine a very different interpretation for Jesus' statement; the "two or three" are not persons. God tells Catherine that the two refers to the two great laws, which Jesus reasserts when a Pharisee asks him about the greatest commandment. Jesus replies, "'You shall love the Lord your God with all your heart, and with all your soul, and with all your mind.' This is the greatest and first commandment. And a second is like it: 'You shall love your neighbor as yourself.' On these two commandments hang all the law and the prophets" (Matt. 22:37-40).

Jesus adapts the first law from Deuteronomy 6:5: "You shall love the LORD your God with all your heart, and with all your soul, and with all your might." The second is from Leviticus 19:18: "You shall not take vengeance or bear a grudge against any of your people, but you shall love your neighbor as yourself: I am the LORD." God gives Moses some additional instruction on this verse's meaning.

> If there is among you anyone in need, a member of your community in any of your towns within the land that the LORD your God is giving you, do not be hard-hearted or tight-fisted toward your needy neighbor. You should rather open your hand, willingly lending enough to meet the need, whatever it may be (Deut. 15:7-8).

Jesus' response to the Pharisee does not introduce two new laws. The Pharisees of his day know both. But the six words between these two directives—*And a second is like it*—reveal the fact that the first law is not above the second. We do not first perfect our love for God and then, once we have got that down, begin love our neighbor. God frequently tells Catherine that she will see every virtue and every vice put into action through her treatment of her neighbors. In fact, without our neighbors, we would find it difficult to love God. This is why God has put us among one another.

God loved us first; in fact, God loved us into existence. Any love we give in return, in a sense, we owe to God. Our love for God is reactive love. The Creator loves us without expectation of recognition, reciprocity, or reward. We don't *have* to love God back if we don't want to. The only way we can love as God loves is to love other people in the same way. We must also love without any expectation of recognition, reciprocity, or reward. God tells Catherine that if we do this, God will accept this as love for God. "The two commandments are to love Me above everything, and your neighbor as yourself, which two are the beginning, the middle and the end of the Law."[1]

Accepting that love for God and neighbor are the same, we still have not defined what we mean by *love*. What does it mean to love our neighbor? The ancient Greek culture identified different kinds of love. *Eros* is the love of lovers. It evokes the concepts of attraction, passion, and longing. *Philia* is affection or deep friendship. *Agape* is the closest approximation to Christian love—love offered regardless of relationship or circumstance.

The first letter of John captures the centrality of love: "Beloved, let us love one another, because love is from God; everyone who loves is born of God and knows God. Whoever does not love does not know God, for God is love" (4:7-8). This is the kind of love that we must offer our neighbor, the kind that is "of God." This love is the root of the tree of the soul—and our life in God. We cannot have life in God—neither in this life nor in the next—without agape. Just as a tree needs water to survive, our soul cannot survive without this love.

Many spiritual writers and thinkers have explored how we understand love. Love has been defined as action that is best for someone else, an effort unselfishly directed toward others. It has also been suggested that love is indiscriminate, offered to all—as Jesus loved. Finally, love is gratuitous, asking or expecting nothing in return—like Jesus. God tells Catherine that this love leads to eternal life.[2]

Because we love in so many ways and with so much nuance in meaning, I propose an alternate word that I believe best captures the principles of the Greek word *agape*: *compassion*. Compassion is a desire to bring peace or healing to those who are suffering or in need. We often see people on the streets asking for compassion; this occurred in Jesus' time as well. Two thousand years ago, people sought compassion for their leprosy, their blindness, or their paralysis. They found compassion in Jesus. Today, people still cry out, "Have mercy on me!" But instead of calling out to Jesus, sometimes they are calling out to us. Today they are asking for compassion for their hunger or their homelessness. The details have changed, but the basic challenge remains the same.

For most of us, compassion occurs naturally within us. Some folks unlearn it through conditioning and training as they age, but children seem to understand it. I believe that when Jesus says, "Unless you change and become like children, you will never enter the kingdom of heaven" (Matt. 18:3), he gives us a clue about the importance of compassion. The desire to offer healing or peace when we are confronted with suffering arises naturally in the humble soul but is neglected by the prideful heart.

One winter, when my two children were five and three years old, I took them to the mountains with an old friend. I was giving my wife a child-free weekend and exposing the kids to a bit of snow. The kids and I got a late start, and I was just a few blocks away from picking up my friend at about 9 p.m. I was crossing under the freeway on H Street, and Sarah, the five-year-old, looked out her window and noticed a woman wrapped in large blankets, standing on the concrete sidewalk next to a shopping cart that probably contained everything she owned. It was January and cold—facts that were not lost on Sarah. I also saw this woman, but I was focused on waiting for the light to change, picking up my friend, and thinking about the drive. I saw her, but didn't really think about her. Sarah asked, "Daddy, why is that person just standing there?"

After a few minutes, I figured out how to explain the issue so that her five-year-old mind could understand it. I said to her, "Sarah, you know how Mommy and Daddy and you and your brother live together in a house? Well, not everyone has a house."

Sarah paused before responding and then asked, "Daddy, will she sleep there tonight?"

"Yes, Sarah. She might sleep there tonight."

"Daddy?"

I closed my eyes and sighed. "Yes, Sarah?"

"It's cold."

"I know, sweetheart. You're right; it is cold."

"Daddy?"

I knew where this was going. "Yes, Sarah?"

"We have an extra room." And she was right. Our house was not large, but it contained four bedrooms. The kids each had a room, and Anne and I shared a room. The fourth room was an extra. For most of the years that we lived there, we kept an extra bed in that room. I think I sighed again and tried to explain.

"Sarah, sometimes the people who don't have houses need more than just houses. Sometimes they need medical help. And sometimes they need more than we can give. My first obligation is to make sure that you and Nick and your mother have a home that is safe."

I was trying to make the point that bringing a stranger into our home could be risky. I struggled with the argument myself. I knew that what I was saying was true, but I still didn't feel good saying it. Certainly children don't always understand the complexities of the decisions that adults have to make. My point here is that Sarah's first reaction was compassion. She recognized a situation in which someone was suffering, and she wanted to help. Her desire may have been naïve, but it arose naturally from her total focus on someone else's need. She was too young to be worried about or even aware of the practical challenges and possible dangers of taking a homeless person into our home. Her reaction illustrates precisely the naiveté that allows children to be compassionate and one of the reasons Jesus wants us to be more like them.

Summary

- The two great laws rely upon each other—we love God through loving our neighbor.
- Compassion is the heart of God's law of love, and it has the following four characteristics: an awareness of what others need, the desire to bring peace or healing to those who suffer, a motivation to give, a lack of discrimination when it comes to helping others.

Prayer

When focusing on compassion, pray for the grace to see others as Jesus sees them. Compassion is built into the Lord's Prayer: "Thy kingdom come, thy will be done on earth as it is in heaven." As you say these words, open your mind to heaven's love for your neighbors who are suffering. "Lead us not into temptation" can also be a call to compassion. You may be tempted to close your eyes, subdue your feelings, or rationalize your failure to act. When seeing those in need, you may be tempted to say, "Get a job," or "They're just lazy." You may be tempted, in fact, to blame them for their suffering.

When reflecting on moments when you have suffered, ask God to open the eyes of your soul to your brothers and sisters before you. The petition "And forgive us our trespasses, as we forgive those who trespass against us" reminds you to act compassionately and mercifully toward others, just as you seek compassion and mercy from God.

O God, open my eyes, mind, and heart and grant me a compassionate spirit. Amen.

For Reflection

You can practice compassion anywhere and anytime by focusing on someone else's need and your reaction to it. You can also explore the depth of your desire to help those who are suffering.

Ask yourself the following questions: To what extent am I noticing the suffering or needs of others? willing to offer help without reward or recognition? willing to help anyone in need regardless of my preconceived notions?

As you reflect, be careful not to judge your reaction. Don't say to yourself, *That was a bad answer* or *I should have done better.* Your goal is to become more aware of your internal reaction to your neighbor in need. Jesus doesn't ask for a guilty conscience; he asks for a compassionate heart.

PART III

STRENGTH

From the foundation of humility and compassion, the tree of our soul emerges from the ground and begins to grow. It becomes visible to the world. As it emerges, it must immediately contend with the environment. We don't live in a vacuum; we live in the real world. The next two chapters will focus on our environment and the strength our soul needs to grow in those conditions.

CHAPTER FIVE

POWERS *of the* SOUL

Let's imagine a young, newly planted tree. Its trunk is narrow and flexible. Often landscapers will drive long stakes or poles into the ground and tie trees to them to strengthen them against the wind. We've seen trees blown down by the wind. The tree of our soul also needs strength and protection from the environment. God identifies for Catherine four winds that sway the tree of soul: the wind of prosperity, the wind of fear, the wind of adversity, and the wind of conscience.[1]

The Wind of Prosperity

When life seems easy and good things are coming our way, we may find ourselves experiencing hidden dangers. One danger involves giving ourselves credit for the abundance—a danger that feeds our pride. A second danger is our dependence on the abundance for our happiness. We let our possessions become too important to us. Because we depend on them for our happiness, we create an opening for the second wind.

The Wind of Fear

When we see difficulty on the horizon—the tide of prosperity turning—we begin to cling to our belongings. We fear losing what we have, whether a possession, a position, or a reputation. We can't enjoy the goodness in our lives while we have it because our attention is focused on our impending loss. This fear robs us of our joy in the present moment because we worry about a future we cannot control. Jesus cautions us about this by saying, "Do not worry about tomorrow, for tomorrow will bring worries of its own. Today's trouble is enough for today" (Matt. 6:34).

The Wind of Adversity

If the trouble we feared finally arrives, it takes away the attachments that we believe we need to be happy, and we suffer. God tells Catherine that the will alone is the source of suffering. We suffer because during the time of prosperity we depend upon possessions for our happiness and we fall into the trap of believing we cannot be happy without them. If we convince ourselves that we are of the earth, believing that earthly things satisfy us, when adversity steals these attachments from us, we will suffer.

I have felt the winds of adversity in my own life, and in one case, I created that hurricane myself. I served as a Catholic school principal and assistant superintendent for fifteen years. I was not aware of how much I had come to identify with those roles. In 2006, I took a new job that drew more upon my teaching and writing skills, but I was not in a formal leadership position. Over time, I became increasingly dissatisfied at work. I kept looking for other work—both within and outside the company—that would get me back to that role. I was heavily invested in that image of myself; my identity was tied to a leadership role. I had convinced myself somewhere along the way that I could not be happy unless I was doing that work. I had let my desire to be in charge become so ingrained to me that when I gave up that role, I suffered—by my own hand.

The Wind of Conscience

Not all wind is bad. We celebrate a gentle breeze that cools us on a hot summer day. God promises Catherine of this good wind. Through the wind of conscience, God prods us to move away from a reliance on worldly possessions and physical pleasure to a reliance on heaven's supreme goodness.

The winds of prosperity, fear, and adversity affect all of us. They are not evil; they are simply part of this human life. We experience them in varying degrees, and no one can avoid them. In fact, God tells Catherine early in *The Dialogue* that "No one born passes this life without pain, bodily or mental."[2] The hardships we face are not the measure of our relationship with God. Instead, our response to life defines that relationship. God assures Catherine that our spirit can rise above challenges because God gives us the two great laws and the three powers of the soul.

In chapter four, we discussed how the word *two* represents the two great laws. In this chapter, we will discuss the second half of "where two or three are gathered in my name." God tells Catherine that the word *three* refers to the three powers of the soul. "The soul I created in My image and similitude, giving her memory, intellect, and will."[3]

Memory

Memory, the first of the three powers, allows us to recall the "blessings and [God's] goodness to the soul."[4] Counting our blessings is certainly not a new idea. When I count my blessings, I usually include good health and employment. Sometimes what we consider a blessing could be better described as good fortune. For example, after my wife and I became engaged, she bought several raffle tickets for the Pheasant Festival at the parish where she was baptized and where we were later married. She bought tickets every year. That year, she won the grand prize—access to a condo on Maui for seven days. Honeymoon question solved. I always thought of that as a blessing, and it was. But look again at the phrase that God uses with Catherine. What does God mean by blessings and goodness to the soul?

Jesus tells us, "It is the spirit that gives life, the flesh is useless. The words that I have spoken to you are spirit and life" (John 6:63). Our spirit is his chief concern. In the story of paying taxes to Caesar, Jesus suggests that we have to live on two levels. (See Matthew 22:15-22.) We have to deal with matters of the flesh. We need food, shelter, and clothing to live. We have to render unto Caesar the things that are his. We have to deal with wealth and poverty and the challenges those bring. But Jesus is telling us there is more to this life than our physical being.

George MacDonald, whom C. S. Lewis recognized as his mentor, suggests that the beginning of the Gospel of John— "What has come into being in him was life" (1:3-4)—does not refer to Jesus' human life. The life in him is not biological life but rather Jesus' life in God—his spiritual, noncorporeal life.[5] God calls us to this life. This is the life that was and is the "light of all people" (John 1:4). The blessings to our soul, then, are those that

70

speak to this spiritual part of us. Through the gift and power of memory, we reconnect to God when we focus on such blessings. Moments of insight or revelation bring us to the threshold of holiness and offer experiences that give us hope and open us to faith in the Divine.

We become spiritually stronger when we cultivate this ability to recall blessings, and we weaken our spirit when we hang on to memories that we should let go. God tells Catherine more than once that "the feet carry the body as the affection carries the soul."[6] God uses this phrase to explain that what we choose to dwell on impacts our soul. This is why disciples of Jesus must guard their thoughts. We cannot always choose our thoughts; we cannot control thoughts that come to us unbidden. However, we can decide to abandon thoughts we no longer wish to pursue. When we focus on thoughts that are not good for us, our souls move away from God.

This may be what Jesus means when he says, "For where your treasure is, there your heart will be also" (Matt. 6:21). The power of the mind to focus on our blessings or on less savory memories impacts our relationship with God. If we focus our memory on blessings, we help direct our spirit toward God's grace. We distance ourselves from God's grace when we give our affection to the wrong things. Why do we do that?

Sometimes we fool ourselves into believing that the thing we want is good for us because it's new, exciting, or thrilling. As God tells Catherine, the object of our desire "so dazzles the eye of the intellect that it can discern and see nothing but such glittering objects. It is the very brightness of the things that causes the intellect to perceive them and the affection to love them; for had worldly things no such brightness there would be no sin, for man, by his nature, cannot desire anything but good, and vice, appearing to man thus, under color of the soul's good, causes him to sin."[7]

Memory is a powerful gift. God's instruction has been borne out by psychological research on happiness. We receive benefit from recalling the blessings in our lives. I recently took the challenge of coming up with three things for which I was grateful every day for twenty-one days in a row. No repeats. I admit I did not do it every day, but I did make sure that within twenty-one days I had named sixty-three blessings for which I was grateful. Each day I named my blessings, I felt happier, and I got better at it. This reveals to us the importance of consistent practice. The more we do something, the better we get at it. I certainly could not have sat down and dashed off a list of sixty-three things in a single sitting, but three a day was completely doable. At first, I thought the no-repeats rule would make it hard, but I was able to identify new sources of gratitude each time. I became more creative and more open-minded about blessings great and small that surrounded me.

Going through this process reminded me of stories that made me laugh, stories that I wanted to share with others. Some research suggests that whether we force ourselves to laugh or laugh in response to a joke, our brain cannot tell the difference. The same endorphins are released if the laugh is contrived or spontaneous. I suspect that in the same way, the blessings to our soul have equal power whether we experience them or recall them. Our memory allows us to relive the blessings we have received. The memory may be the laughter of good times, the tears of grief for lost love, or the warmth of a tender moment.

We may have difficulty taking the time to do daily memory work. In this age of information—or age of technology, as some call it—the amount of information that we create, share, and absorb every day increases exponentially every year. I would call this time the age of distraction. Television shows, movies, social and professional networks, and personal digital devices demand so much of our attention that we have precious little time to be alone with our thoughts. And yet we all need time to reflect on God's blessings. Instead of offering a generic list of spiritual blessings, I would like to share two of the blessings to my soul that are dearest to me.

I Am Loved

Many years ago, when my wife, Anne, and I were engaged but not yet married, we drove through California's central valley. We fell into a deep discussion that was challenging for me. I explained some serious issues from my past that I thought might be unsettling to her. When I finished recounting my story, I felt vulnerable, and Anne was quiet for some time. Finally, I said, "Please say something." I was fully prepared for her to say, "Stop the car. I'm getting out." Okay, maybe that's overly dramatic, but I wouldn't have been surprised if she'd said, "I need time to think about this."

To my surprise, Anne did not say either of those things. Instead, she said these words: "I really love you." Sitting with that response in silence, I was overwhelmed. A tear formed in the corner of my eye and rolled down my cheek. I cannot remember now if she asked me about the tear, but I believe that she did. I said to her, "If you can love me after what I've just told you, then it must be possible that God also loves me." I believe that was the first time I knew in my heart and soul that I was loved by God. To this day, this story remains one of my most powerful spiritual memories.

Singing God's Praise

I am a musician—I play the guitar. Since I was about fourteen, music has been an enormous part of my life, for which I am grateful. I was lucky enough to be part of a choir for the four years I lived in Reno. Two particular moments in the choir will stay with me forever. The first was singing "O Holy Night" at midnight Mass on Christmas Eve. The sound that we were making in the church, leading an entire community in this beautiful song, was emotionally powerful. I remember feeling almost dizzy.

Some years later, we sang a song titled "No Greater Love" for the Easter Vigil. At one point in the song, we silenced the instruments and sang a cappella in four-part harmony. Our harmonies were tight, and the song was deeply moving. One parishioner told me after the service that we made her cry. Singing to God, about God, in a church full of people who believe in God can be emotionally and spiritually overwhelming. This song certainly was a blessing and a moment of grace for me. Though twenty years ago now, I still tell this story to my children. I tell them about the experience and its impact on me. As I do, I relive the joy of that experience, and it continues to be a blessing in my life. It triggers a feeling of deep gratitude for that time and place in my life along with the people with whom I sang. I treasure it still.

My stories provide two examples, but I believe we can experience many different blessings to the soul. We may find blessing in being truly happy for another person, in creating a friendly or romantic relationship that we can cherish, in laughing until it hurts or heals, or in believing we are truly forgiven. Though the blessings differ, they all have one similarity: Each is an internal experience. Blessings to the soul happen on the inside. This doesn't mean that good fortune or material blessings aren't real blessings, but God directs Catherine to focus on the work of the soul. In order to grow spiritually, we must remember the blessings to our soul—the profound moments of our lives that touch us at a deep spiritual level. These moments bring us joy. They reignite our gratitude for the many blessings we've been given, renew our trust in the Lord, and give us strength to endure hardship. The blessings to our soul fill a reservoir with joy and faith that we can draw upon every day.

Understanding

God introduces understanding, also referred to as *intellect*, as "the most noble aspect of the soul."[8] For God, understanding includes rationality but is more than that. Spiritual understanding is not reason alone but reason coupled with faith. God uses the eye as an analogy to explain the role of understanding. We all know what our eyes do. They perceive images. Just as a camera needs a flash to be of any use in the dark, we need light in order to see. For both sight and understanding, we use the term *perceive*. Our eyes perceive the physical world, and our souls perceive the spiritual world. But the intellect, like the eye, does not produce its own light. It requires an external light source. The intellect is the eye of the soul, but it cannot see without the light of faith.[9] Reason alone cannot lead us to faith; rather, reason with faith leads us to spiritual understanding.

In chapter two, we discussed the two overarching characteristics of God's nature that we should try to know: divine goodness and mercy. Jesus models these attributes for us. God grants us understanding—the ability to comprehend through faith and reason—so that we may understand Jesus. God declares to Catherine that the purpose of understanding is "to gaze into the ineffable love" revealed to us by Jesus "so that, in Him, you behold the fire of My charity."[10] God describes this charity as unfathomable—"the fire and abyss of My inestimable love."[11] Later God adds that understanding through faith enables us to discern, know, and follow the teachings of Jesus. God describes the teaching and example of Jesus as a road that Jesus builds for us "by His actions, giving you His doctrine by example rather than by words; for He practiced, first Himself, what He afterwards taught you."[12] Jesus' teachings lead us to God. "For with the eye of the intellect illuminated by . . . faith, [the soul] sees Me, the Infinite and Eternal Good, whom [the soul] hopes to obtain by grace."[13]

So how do we know Jesus? The answer is twofold. First, God affirms that Jesus and the Almighty are one. We cannot know God without knowing ourselves, and, by extension, we can conclude that we also cannot know Jesus without knowing ourselves. Second, we need to know about Jesus. Therefore, a deep knowledge of the Gospels is central to exercising this power of the soul. We build our foundation of knowledge upon reading and reflecting on the life, teachings, passion, and resurrection of Jesus. We cannot understand Jesus if we do not know his story. Through reading scripture, we can reflect on Jesus' response to the people he encounters and compare them to our own intentions and actions. Perhaps this understanding made the acronym WWJD—What Would Jesus Do?—popular with modern Christians. We know Jesus is the standard, and we cannot answer the WWJD question without immersing ourselves in the Gospels. In them, we find again and again what Jesus offers: unending mercy, forgiveness, compassion, and a fierce dedication to the will of God.

Will

God explains to Catherine three characteristics of our will. First, the will exercises the power of choice. Our choices and actions can lead to a life of grace or suffering. The desires of this world ultimately do not satisfy us. They leave us, in fact, empty. More than one spiritual master has suggested that if we believe we are created by God in God's image and with God's Spirit within us, ultimately only God can satisfy our longing. So the will—our power to choose—must deliberately pursue thoughts and actions that are consistent with our desire to live a life in God. Christianity challenges us to make the will of God our first desire. When understanding keeps Jesus as its main focus, our soul is better prepared to choose God.

Second, exercising our will requires two components: reason and freedom. Both of these can be compromised. Reason can be constrained by strong emotions or lack of knowledge. We've felt the discomfort of having to make choices when we don't have all the information or do not fully understand the situation. Freedom can be constrained by desire, which can capture our will and enslave us. Desire compels us to think and act in ways that we would not if desire were absent. When either or both are compromised, we may make choices that lead us away from God. God tells Catherine that the soul cannot want bad things.[14] If that's true, how do we make bad choices?

In retrospect, poor choices always seem obvious to us, but we may not recognize them in the moment. We may not know when our reason and freedom are compromised. The choice between a decision that is good or one that is bad or unwise isn't always clear. Impulses, powerful emotions, and intense desires can deceive us. Sometimes the world's pleasures delude us, tricking us into believing the wrong choices will make us happy. They confuse us because they appear to us as something good when they are not. For these reasons, self-knowledge is critical to the appropriate exercise of the will. We have to work hard to become aware of the desires within us that restrict our freedom.

Third, the will is manifested in action. "Every work, good or bad, is done by means of the body."[15] Or as Jesus tells us, "Each tree is known by its fruit" (Luke 6:44). Here's a simple example.

Thought: I want to exercise today.

Will: I get in the car, drive to the gym, sit at the bench press machine, and start pushing.

Here's another example. My wife and I decided to help the near-homeless youth we once met in a park by thinking through the situation. He did not know where he was going to sleep that night or even how he was going to manage his belongings, which he carried (dragged) in a laundry basket, a duffel bag, and a plastic garbage bag. My wife and I quickly agreed this young man needed help. We exercised our will through the following:

- Talking to him and learning his story
- Offering some advice on finding work in the short term
- Making phone calls and identifying some options for shelter
- Acquiring a large rolling suitcase that met his needs
- Driving him to the Salvation Army
- Giving him some survival money

Exercising our will did not mean making a decision or commitment in our mind. Exercising our will meant taking action.

The Stamina of the Will

Each of us has experienced moments when our willpower didn't have enough power. We've given in to a habit or action we had been trying to avoid. Whether we want to eat better, exercise more, or spend less, we know what it is like to fall off the wagon. The American Psychological Association provides some insight into why this happens. Our willpower acts as a mental muscle. Often, when we exercise our will, we do so to resist temptation. We engage in an internal struggle between conflicting desires. For example, the desire to lose weight versus the desire to eat a tasty cookie. We may be able to strengthen our willpower through exercise, but our will also can become tired. Just as our physical muscles tire in the short term after exercising them, resisting a succession of temptations can drain our capacity to resist subsequent temptations. So if we walk away from the cookie jar nine times a day, we may be too weak to resist the tenth temptation.

Knowing that our willpower can tire like any muscle, we can put three strategies into practice in order to give ourselves a little help. First, we can plan ahead. Deciding on a response in advance can remove some of the effort involved in responding—because we have already decided. Second, we can remember that the idiom *out of sight, out of mind* really works. We don't have to place ourselves in situations we know will be hard to resist. Third, we can call in reinforcements. If we feel our will slipping, we can ask for help or support from a friend or family member.

The Three Together

When we exercise the three powers of the soul in concert, we become a vessel of God's ineffable love—a love beyond all words.

When our memory recalls the blessings we've received, when we focus our understanding on the fire of Jesus' love for us, and when we allow love to direct our will, we grow closer to God, for we know that God is love. God explains it to Catherine in this way:

> When the heart of man is drawn by the affection of love, as I have said, it is drawn together with all the powers of his soul, that is, with the Memory, the Intellect [understanding], and the Will; now, when these three powers are harmoniously joined together in My Name, all the other operations which the man performs, whether in deed or thought, are pleasing, and joined together by the effect of love.[16]

Summary

- As the tree of our soul emerges from the soil, it must contend with the winds of prosperity, adversity, fear, and conscience. To withstand these winds, God gave us three powers that infuse our souls with strength: memory, understanding, and will.
- Memory allows us to recall God's blessings to our souls.
- Understanding allows us to comprehend Jesus. The Gospels help us understand Jesus' inexhaustible compassion for us; Jesus' teachings of the way, the truth, and the life; and Jesus' path, which we can follow to find God's eternal peace and unending grace.
- The will is our power to choose, and if our understanding is focused on Jesus, we may find it easier to choose God.
- Exercising the will requires reason and freedom.
- Exercising the will requires action.
- The will can tire if overtaxed, just like our muscles.

Prayer

First, focus your prayer on letting go of memories that are not good for you. Ask God to replace the memories of temptation with memories of your many blessings. Second, pray for insight from the Gospels that will deepen your understanding of Jesus. Third, pray for the resolve to fuel your willpower with your faith and convictions.

The words of the Lord's Prayer touch on the will: "Thy kingdom come, thy will be done." When you recite the Lord's Prayer, you ask that God will marry your will to God's will. I recently found a note my wife wrote to herself. It simply read, "I want to want what God wants me to want."

As an alternative to the Lord's Prayer, focus on the elements of humility.

God of love, open my eyes to your blessings and give me a grateful heart. Deepen my understanding of Jesus' life, teachings, and resurrection. Strengthen my will and grant me the knowledge and courage to do your will. Amen.

For Reflection

In what ways are you showing gratefulness for the blessings you have received that others may need? reflecting on the depth of Jesus' love for you? allowing God's wisdom to direct your will?

CHAPTER SIX

VIRTUES *of the* SOUL

The three powers of memory, understanding, and will provide sources of mental and spiritual strength. This strength expresses itself in three virtues that God repeatedly references. Patience, perseverance, and courage allow the tree of our soul to weather the winds of prosperity, fear, adversity, and conscience and to live a life pleasing to God.

Patience

Patience is a core virtue of the tree of your soul, and patience is connected to suffering. God tells Catherine, "Patience cannot be proved in any other way than by suffering."[1] If we didn't face hardships in our lives, waiting to overcome such difficulties would not be a challenge and patience would not be necessary. But hardships confront us all. So we have the opportunity to embrace or abandon patience.

Elsewhere in *The Dialogue*, God reminds Catherine that all the virtues are proved by means of our neighbor. "Man proves his patience on his neighbor, when he receives injuries from him."[2]

God makes the case that when our neighbor treats us poorly, we should be patient and not react too quickly.

I have caught myself lacking patience in the checkout line at the grocery store. Perhaps the person in front of me takes a long time. First, he asks for a price check on an item. Then he asks a question about coupons. Then a product is damaged, and a clerk has to go find another one. Then the customer's debit card doesn't work. Inevitably, if I find myself in this situation, I'm in a hurry and need to be somewhere. So I am annoyed with the delay. I start acting impatient. I let out an exasperated sigh. I cross my arms. I roll my eyes and start shifting my stance. I physically display impatience in all kinds of ways. But really, for whose benefit is my posturing? Who does it help? No one. My actions embarrass my neighbor, who probably does not need to be reminded that other people are in line at the grocery store. My actions serve only to reinforce and display for others the thought in my head: *This is taking longer than I want it to.* My impatience is all about me.

God also teaches Catherine that patience flows from humility and is connected to obedience. God asks us to be obedient to the laws of love and to the example of Christ. Obedience requires patience. Children are disobedient when they break a rule their parents have established. Often they do this because they want something and they have difficulty waiting. If they could be patient, they would not have broken the rule. So disobedience can be an expression of impatience. Adults are no different. Our sins can often be described as a failure to wait. When desire or temptation comes, we can choose to respond with action or patience.

When speaking on the virtue of patience, we often think of Job and his legendary portrayal. After losing his family, his fortune, and his health in the first chapter, Job does not give up on

God. "The LORD gave, and the LORD has taken away; blessed be the name of the LORD" (Job 1:21). Job sits upon the ground and waits, all the while attacked by his friends who continually try to convince him—for more than thirty chapters—that he must be guilty of sin. But Job feels confident in his conviction that he is not. He does not know why he is suffering, but he retains a positive attitude toward God. "Even now, in fact, my witness is in heaven, and he that vouches for me is on high" (Job 16:19).

The Secret of Patience

Patience entails waiting with a pleasant attitude. It means having the discipline of Job and not letting the waiting—which we often cannot control—change our behavior or demeanor, which we can control. The patient soul may not get relief any faster than the impatient soul, but the latter will make the waiting a heavier cross to bear. The patient soul can tolerate the delay and maintain a positive attitude. While most of us don't experience Job's dramatic losses all at once, we do sometimes face difficulties for extended periods of time—years or even decades. They can be hard to bear. Yet in these trying times, the greatest gift we can give to ourselves and to those around us is the gift of patience.

Practicing Patience

First, stay calm. Breathe slowly, smile, and be still. We create space for patience by breathing. Breathe through the discomfort because (1) the experience won't last forever, (2) resistance won't change the situation, and (3) judging the experience—labeling it as inconvenient, annoying, or a disaster—won't help.

Persistence

Along with patience, God consistently praises the virtue of persistence, informing Catherine that "perseverance receives the crown of glory and victory in the life everlasting."[3] In a results-oriented world, we may have trouble practicing persistence. We have trained ourselves to expect things to work right away. When we click on an Internet browser, we expect to be connected almost immediately. We seek instant results. But reaching a goal—something we value highly—may not be a quick process. The things that matter most to us usually require sustained effort.

God explains the virtue of persistence with a simple visual story. He grants Catherine a vision of God's divine nature represented by a tree that can be seen from a distance. As souls approach the tree, they encounter a thornbush surrounding the tree at its base, preventing easy access. The thorns symbolize the adversity we often face in letting go of our attachments, the stripping away of the material possessions to which we cling. The thorns provide a useful image for this because thorns hurt. Wishing to avoid the thorns, the souls look around for options.

In the distance, the souls spy a hill that appears to be covered with corn and wheat—a hill without a barrier of thorns. No persistence required. So they leave the tree and head for the food. But what looks like wheat from a distance turns out to be only weeds. We see this happen in our own lives. At first glance or from a distance, an idea or goal may look good and the path toward it easy. So we pursue that goal and immerse ourselves in it. But we learn that the goal looks different up close. Sometimes we don't know how to relinquish our goal. Those who are unwilling to return and push through the thornbush eventually starve among the weeds. Those with the virtue of persistence return to the tree. They push through the thornbush—letting go of the attachments in their lives that are not of God. God's message seems simple enough: If we want to embrace God, we have to let go of everything else. We have to let go of our attachments, which requires persistence.

The Gospel of Luke offers two parables that highlight the virtue of persistence. In Luke 18:1-8, Jesus tells the parable of an unjust judge. This judge is not a nice man; he doesn't fear God or respect people. He's harsh. However, he grants justice to a widow—not because he cares about her or out of any sense of duty—simply because of her persistence. Jesus encourages us not to give up.

Jesus also tells the story of a persistent friend. (See Luke 11:5-10.) We can easily put ourselves into this story. At midnight, the telephone rings. We are asleep, and we have already put our children to bed. The phone call startles us, but we answer with a somewhat groggy hello.

"Hey, sorry to wake you, old friend, but I need a favor," says the voice on the line. We are already thinking, *Friends do not call at midnight and wake up an entire household.* He continues. "Can I borrow some bread and maybe some cheese? I have unexpected family and friends staying with me, and I'm a little low on groceries."

"Now!? Can't this wait until morning?" We hang up.

The phone rings again. Before we can say anything, our friend asks, "Please? It will only take a minute. I can walk over right now."

We know how we will respond. We'll say, "Fine." We will struggle out of bed, gather some food, throw it in a bag, and be at the door when our friend walks up. We may have the grace to be polite when we open the door, but we may not. Jesus makes the argument that we are willing to do this not because of the friendship but because of our friend's persistence. We just want to go back to bed, and we will comply with the request to make it go away. Jesus praises the virtue of persistence.

My son, Nick, practices *parkour*, often defined as "street gymnastics." He works with a trainer. At one time, he was working on a flip. Over and over. Literally head over heels. He could launch, get the height, and turn in the air with no problems. He just could not stick the landing—could not land on his feet and stay there. Week after week he worked on the flip. His coach was watching him, giving him feedback, and demonstrating. One night they decided to analyze Nick's approach. "How many steps are you taking before you launch?" the coach asked. They counted Nick's steps and chose a set pattern. Nick started working with it, and within ten minutes, he stuck the landing. His arms went up, and he let out a *yes*—an *I did it!* He felt great because of the complexity of the challenge and the amount of effort he had put in to overcoming it. Nick's success was a celebration of persistence. If the flip hadn't been hard to do, if Nick had nailed the landing the first time he tried, his achievement would not have been as exciting. Persistence is about the effort we expend to work through a difficulty.

Practicing Persistence

We practice persistence by committing to an action and then doing it. If we feel our prayer life is erratic, we can set a time to pray for just one minute every day. Maybe it's when we wake up, or maybe it's before bed. We may face obstacles: We may be too tired or we may forget. Or worse, we may feel like our prayer is not working—like nothing is happening or changing, like God is not hearing us. We will be tempted to quit. But I believe that we cannot be persistent in big things if we cannot be persistent in small things. So the next time we have a task and want to quit, we can take a deep breath and remind ourselves, *I'm going to keep this promise. I'm going to do what I said I would.* And do it.

Courage

Though God references the virtue of courage less often than the other two virtues, God mentions it in connection with patience or perseverance. Sometimes translated as fortitude, courage is the virtue of deep resolve. Its Anglo-French root means "heart," referring to our innermost feelings. Courage, then, could be understood as the mental or moral strength to withstand fear, damage, hardship, and disappointment. God tells Catherine that pain in life is a given: "No one can pass through this life without a cross."[4] We *know* that life is hard. We will face failures, setbacks, and losses. God assures Catherine that Jesus' life demonstrates how we can live a life of virtue and that courage is given to those who follow "the road of His doctrine."[5]

Practicing Courage

Practicing courage doesn't entail practicing how not to be afraid. We cannot by an act of will stop ourselves from having a feeling we are experiencing. And fear isn't always a hindrance. If we find ourselves in woods that contain bears, fear might inspire us to take precautions to protect ourselves. That would be a reasonable and appropriate response to fear. The courage we are often called upon to exercise is the courage to do the right thing. Standing up for justice requires courage, especially when the forces of injustice are strong and threatening. When telling the truth means admitting our failures or imperfections, we will need courage. We can practice courage by asking ourselves three questions:

1. What am I afraid of and why? Identify the event or action that triggers the fear.
2. What is the fear driving me to do? Identify the actions you are considering.
3. What would I do if I were not afraid?

If this activity seems too hard to do alone, we can seek out a wise and trustworthy friend with whom we can share the fear and gain insight and guidance. After speaking with a friend, we might find that we are perceiving the situation incorrectly or overstating the consequences.

Summary

- Three core virtues create the foundation of our soul's strength: patience, persistence, and courage.
- Patience means having a pleasant attitude and demeanor as we deal with delay and inconvenience.
- Persistence refers to applying consistent effort even when we want to give up.
- Courage involves staying committed to God in our heart and mind, our faith, our morals, and our beliefs despite fear and difficulty.

Prayer

When focusing on the virtues of the soul, the purpose of prayer is not to ask for a life without hardship. Rather, ask for the gifts that will help you best cope with those hardships. You need grace to build up your capacity for patience, persistence, and courage.

In the Lord's Prayer, you say, "Thy kingdom come, thy will be done." This phrase expresses confidence that God will ultimately accomplish God's will. However, these words could also be interpreted as a promise on your part, a promise that you remain open to God's will so that God's purpose can be accomplished through you, so that you can be the hands and feet on earth that will help bring about God's reign. "Thy will be done" may need to be done by you so ask not only for guidance on what to do but also for the patience, persistence, and courage to do it.

God of light, as I move through this day, give me the grace to be patient with others. Strengthen my persistence and courage to do your will in the face of difficulty and fear. Amen.

For Reflection

What (or who) in my life tries my patience the most right now? How can I adopt a better attitude toward that situation or person? What is testing my resolve? Where do I need to persist? What am I avoiding because I am afraid? Where do I need to summon courage to face the difficulty?

PART IV

ACTION

In Part I, we explored the circle of knowledge of self and knowledge of God. In Part II, we reflected on our tree's foundation and the need to ensure the tree is planted in the soil of humility where the roots of compassion grow strong. In Part III, the tree of our soul moved above ground, and we began to feel the winds of adversity. Then, the tree found its strength in the powers and virtues of the soul.

We have focused our work internally thus far—the mind, heart, and spirit. This section will discuss decision and action—how we respond to the world around us. Our response is our testament, our declaration of faith through action. Remember that every virtue (and every vice) is proved by means of our neighbor. We all have virtuous thoughts. We see opportunities for humility, compassion, understanding, or patience toward our neighbor. But if those thoughts don't translate into action, perhaps we never really understood the virtues in the first place. Real virtue leaves evidence behind.

CHAPTER SEVEN

DISCERNMENT

What is discernment? Secular definitions indicate that it means "to perceive and judge well." This might lead us to conclude that discernment is merely a logical process. Spiritual discernment, however, requires more than logical decision making; spiritual discernment enables our soul to determine how best to act when we encounter a situation with moral or spiritual implications. In such situations, we must discern whether to act and what action to take. At the conclusion of the metaphor of the tree of the soul, God tells Catherine that all the fruits of the soul are born of discernment.[1] Later, God articulates for Catherine the importance and power of discernment:

> [Discernment is] that light which dissipates all darkness, takes away ignorance, and is the condiment of every instrument of virtue. Holy discretion [discernment] is a prudence which cannot be cheated, a fortitude which cannot be beaten, a perseverance from end to end, stretching from Heaven to earth, that is, from knowledge of Me to knowledge of self, and from love of Me to love of others.[2]

Discernment, then, provides a culmination and integration of every aspect of the tree of the soul. It is a thoughtful and prayerful practice of reflection that brings our entire being—heart, mind, soul, and strength—to bear on problems we face. Marshaling all the parts of ourselves can take time, and certainly some of the more significant decisions we face deserve this time because discernment asks us to consider the following:

- What we ought to do may be in conflict with our own desires so we must be informed by knowledge of self and a clear awareness of our own feelings, thoughts, and desires.
- If we want our discernment to lead to an expression of God's will, our process must be informed by knowledge of God.
- To act appropriately, we may need to get past our judgmental thoughts, which requires a degree of humility.
- The law of love requires our action to be compassionate.
- The circumstances of our problem may overwhelm us with sadness or make us question our faith. We can draw upon our powers of memory, understanding, and will to persevere.
- The action to which our discernment leads us may be arduous. The virtues of patience, persistence, and courage help us withstand hardship.

The book of James offers valuable insight for preparing for the process of discernment: "The wisdom from above is first pure, then peaceable, gentle, willing to yield, full of mercy and good fruits, without a trace of partiality or hypocrisy" (3:17). This text reinforces some of the ideas God discusses with Catherine including acting with mercy (compassion), dropping our assumptions (knowledge of self), and yielding good fruits. It also introduces three key ideas not yet discussed that can prepare the soul for discernment: calm, willingness to yield, and integrity.

Calm

We don't make our best choices when we feel agitated. Our best choices usually come when we are at peace. When we are overly influenced by short-term emotions and conflicted feelings, our decision-making skills suffer. While our feelings do provide important information, we need to balance them with other considerations. If we are experiencing intense emotions toward a problem, we may need some distance from it.

One way to do that is to look at the situation from the perspective of a person whose judgment we trust. This may be why the phrase WWJD, which I mentioned earlier, appeals to us. Certainly, we trust Jesus, and thinking about Jesus' actions always helps me remember the two great laws: love God and love neighbor. But sometimes we need more guidance when confronted with twenty-first century problems, many of which the Gospels do not address. In addition to Jesus, we can choose a role model from those we know well. We can ask ourselves, *Who of my friends makes good judgments? Who is wise? Who is spiritually strong? Who is my Solomon?* Once I have chosen a person, I ponder what he or she would say about the situation. This simple shift in perspective allows us to recognize our emotional reactions without letting them overwhelm us.

Willingness to Yield

If we describe ourselves as having a willingness to yield, we may think that means we don't try to win arguments. But more is implied. A better way to describe this characteristic might be keeping ourselves open to reason. Being willing to yield involves seeking counsel, listening to others, opening ourselves to other perspectives.

Here's an example. A young woman accepted a proposal of marriage. Her mother was extremely concerned and did not agree with her daughter's decision. The mother came to me with the dilemma. She felt she could not attend the wedding; she would be acting hypocritically to witness the union when she did not support it. Yet the mother also knew that not attending could seriously damage her relationship with her daughter.

The mother's situation called for discernment because of the challenge of her conflicting values. Her dilemma was mired in judgment about the groom, beliefs about sacramental marriage, a commitment to the tenets of Christian faith, a concern for personal integrity, and deep feelings for her daughter. The mother and I talked about her options—attending versus not attending—and the impact each would have on her daughter and other family members.

Ultimately, the mother's decision came down to an understanding of which beliefs or values would take precedence. Which would guide her in choosing a course of action? If personal integrity or religious teaching came first, she would not attend but risk damaging her relationship with her daughter. If concern for protecting that relationship came first, she would attend but risk not acting consistently with her own beliefs and values. The mother and I spoke at length, but she did not make a decision in my presence. She left saying, "I need to think and pray about this." She spoke with others in her life whom she trusted as well. In the end, she chose to share her thinking with her daughter as delicately as possible and attend the wedding.

This mother modeled the practice of seeking counsel and being open to the thoughts of others. Getting second (and third and fourth) opinions is not a new idea. The Bible tells us, "Listen to advice and accept instruction, that you may gain wisdom for the future" (Prov. 19:20). We need one another on the spiritual journey. None of us is smart enough by ourselves to know the answers to all life's questions. We need to listen to one another, challenge one another, and occasionally assure one another that we're not crazy. By listening to and talking with people whose judgment we trust, we enjoy a wealth of experience that can guide us in the path of wisdom.

Integrity

We show integrity when our beliefs, words, and actions match and work together. In other words, no hypocrisy. In the Gospel of Matthew, Jesus chides the Pharisees for their lack of integrity.

> "Woe to you, scribes and Pharisees, hypocrites! For you clean the outside of the cup and of the plate, but inside they are full of greed and self-indulgence. You blind Pharisee! First clean the inside of the cup, so that the outside also may become clean.
>
> "Woe to you, scribes and Pharisees, hypocrites! For you are like whitewashed tombs, which on the outside look beautiful, but inside they are full of the bones of the dead and of all kinds of filth. So you also on the outside look righteous to others, but inside you are full of hypocrisy and lawlessness" (23:25-28).

Our external behavior should match our internal beliefs. When we find ourselves in the process of discernment, we must ask, *Is the response I am considering consistent with what I profess to believe?* If not, our response may not be well received. Integrity establishes credibility. Jesus can speak and act the way he does because he walks the talk. He shows compassion, offers forgiveness, and lives his life in total devotion to the will of God. Jesus can ask others to leave their lives behind and follow him because he has already left everything to follow God. In the same way, we can give only advice that we follow or encourage behavior that we model.

Summary

- Discernment involves every level of the tree of the soul.
- Preparation for discernment includes the following:
  - Being calm—balancing our emotional reactions with prayer and patience
  - Being willing to yield—actively seeking counsel and listening to others' advice
  - Demonstrating integrity—ensuring that how we speak and act is consistent with our professed beliefs

Prayer

By beginning the process of discernment with prayer, you open yourself to divine wisdom. "If any of you is lacking in wisdom, ask God, who gives to all generously and ungrudgingly, and it will be given you" (James 1:5). This instruction is consistent with Jesus' promise: "How much more will the heavenly Father give the Holy Spirit to those who ask him!" (Luke 11:13).

In praying for discernment, follow the humble example of Solomon.

"O LORD my God, you have made me your servant king in place of my father David, although I am only a little child. I do not know how to go out or come in. And your servant is in the midst of the people whom you have chosen, a great people, so numerous they cannot be numbered or counted. Give your servant therefore an understanding mind to govern your people, able to discern between good and evil" (1 Kings 3:7-9).

In response to Solomon's prayer, God grants him wisdom that had not been seen before and that none who would follow him would exhibit. Solomon's humble appeal for wisdom pleases God.

When you say the Lord's Prayer, "Thy will be done" echoes the conclusion of Jesus' prayer at Gethsemane: "Yet not what I want but what you want" (Matt. 26:39). To me, Jesus' words act as an appeal for wisdom and courage. You seek God's wisdom so that you can know what God wants. You place your will at God's disposal, offering to be a vessel of God's will.

Holy God, I need your grace today. I am concerned about _____.
But my knowledge is limited, and my understanding is incomplete.
You know all things. Open my heart and mind to your wisdom.
Grant me a sense of calm, a willingness to yield, and the gift of
integrity. Teach me to act rightly for your glory. Amen.

For Reflection

To what extent are you able to remain calm when discerning? Who are the people you consult when you need a second opinion? What are the qualities of those people? How important is integrity to you? To what extent do you notice hypocrisy in others but not yourself?

CHAPTER EIGHT

FRUITS *of the* SOUL

Discernment leads to action. The disciple whose soul is grounded in knowledge of self and God, rich in humility and compassion, and strong in virtue produces fruit. God specifically lists four main fruits of the tree of the soul: charity, prayer, sharing our faith, and the example of a holy life.

Charity

God names charity the greatest virtue and one of two virtues that constitute our mutual debt to our neighbor. God explicitly tells Catherine that "charity gives life to all the virtues, because no virtue can be obtained without charity, which is the pure love of Me."[1] In other words, charity is the motive for all virtues because all virtues ultimately flow from love. Charity is the expression of the love of God and neighbor. As we discussed in chapter four, these two loves are one. Any act done on behalf of our neighbor that is an expression of love is charity, whether it's financial help, listening, or even a hug.

We see this understanding of charity in the teachings of Jesus. Consider the answer Jesus gives when asked, "Who is my neighbor?" (Luke 10:29). The parable of the good Samaritan illustrates our obligation to be vessels of mercy and compassion to people who suffer regardless of the color of their skin, the country of their origin, the language they speak, or even the faith they profess. (See Luke 10:29-37.) Those characteristics of others are irrelevant to our obligation to be compassionate and charitable.

In our attempts to act charitably, we are often met with challenges. In December 2012, I went to San Francisco, California, for a five-day conference. Each day, as I walked from the hotel to the conference site, the city presented me with many opportunities to give. On every street corner, I encountered several people, apparently homeless, asking for help. The days were cold and often rainy. The sight of people in need tugged at my heartstrings. I didn't feel right giving nothing, but I also could not help them all. So I tried each day to give at least once. One fellow shook my hand to thank me when I gave him five dollars, but then he wouldn't let go and demanded more. That situation scared me. Once I gave two dollars to a man, and the fellow standing next to him asked, "What about me?" I was caught off guard, so I replied, "You two can share." One evening I called my wife and said, "I could give away my entire paycheck this week. And though it might be appreciated, it wouldn't really change anything."

Most of us have had similar experiences. Sometimes we give and sometimes we don't—both for myriad reasons. When I have reflected on my own experience and compared my emotional reaction to not helping with my intellectual doubt about whether the need was real, I always come to the same conclusion: Walking away because I doubt someone's need does not satisfy me. I have given enough times to know that the decision to help usually feels right to me, and I am able to dismiss any doubt as unimportant. Following the gospel requires letting go of our doubts. They are not our first concern.

Charity begins with awareness—really seeing our brothers and sisters. Once we are aware of the adversities they face, the second element of charity arises: We are moved to act compassionately. Knowing the suffering others face and desiring to alleviate that suffering lead us to the third aspect of charity: capacity. Our capacity—or ability to act—is always changing. Some days we can give money, and others days our wallet is empty. But charity is not just about money. If we cannot offer money, we can offer time, attention, a listening ear, or a hug. Some days we don't have strength or emotional energy even to smile at a homeless person. In these moments, I benefit most from my little acts of charity. I feel better when I offer kindness to others. In this way, charity is a gift we give ourselves.

Jesus tells his disciples, "You received without payment; give without payment" (Matt. 10:8). Everything we have—our possessions, our livelihood, our friends and family, our faith, even our lives—has been given to us free of charge. The Lord of the harvest sends us out into the vineyard to share what has been freely given. Charity is gratitude in action.

Forgiveness as Charity

While God does not specifically mention forgiveness as one of the fruits of the soul, I believe it is perhaps one of the most critical expressions of the charitable attitude God wants us to have for our neighbor. For many years, the hardest part of practicing forgiveness for me was trying to understand what forgiveness was and how it worked.

We find one of the best Gospel stories for demonstrating the concept of forgiveness in Luke 7, the story of the woman washing Jesus' feet. (See Luke 7:36-50.) This story is recounted in all four Gospels, but Luke's version is unique in that the Gospel writer implies that the woman is sinful. This woman demonstrates three characteristics that we have already covered. The first is humility. When she arrives at the house of the Pharisee, the woman has already judged herself. She knows that she needs forgiveness, and she humbles herself before Jesus in a dramatic and highly visible way. The woman also demonstrates the virtue of courage. To go to the house of the Pharisee whom she knows will judge her harshly—he makes it clear that he wants her out of the house—is brave to say the least. Finally, she demonstrates hope. She comes before Jesus because she already believes that Jesus will accept her and forgive her. Now, some may argue that hers is an act of simple desperation and that she doesn't really know that she will be forgiven. But I contend that if she wasn't pretty confident about Jesus, she would not risk the humiliation and shame. Like this woman, a truly penitent person demonstrates humility, courage, and hope.

How do these actions lead to forgiveness? How does forgiveness work? What does it mean? I've asked many people these questions and received different answers. The most common response I hear is that phrase "forgive and forget." This answer has never satisfied me for two reasons. First, why use the word *forgive* to define *forgiveness?* Second, in my experience, we never truly forget the offenses that require forgiveness. If we are gracious, we may never bring them up again, but that's different than forgetting altogether. I cannot say I have forgotten the times when others have hurt me, but I have tried to let go of the hurt. And although others have forgiven me, I have never been able to purge my greatest failures from my memory. I can count them all.

Perhaps we overuse the word *forgive*. We know Jesus forgives sins. He forgives the woman who washes his feet, noting that her sins were many. (See Luke 7:47.) He forgives the soldiers who crucify him saying, "Father, forgive them; for they do not know what they are doing" (Luke 23:34). But sometimes when we say, "I forgive you," we are forgiving someone for accidentally breaking a dish. We forgive our friends and colleagues for not showing up for a lunch date, or we forgive our children for spilling the milk. I believe that imprecise language challenges us in these situations. We do not respond to regret for an accident or forgetfulness differently from how we respond to harm caused on purpose. In both cases we hear, "I'm sorry," and it elicits the same response: "I forgive you." This seems appropriate on the surface, but using the word *forgive* for unintended harm robs the word of its power to accept contrition for harm by intent.

We need to distinguish between two similar but separate concepts. The first is being gracious in reacting to harm by accident. In this case, the resolution requires restitution as a demonstration of responsibility. I attended a high school that was a few miles from my home. I usually was able to arrange a carpool, but some days I could not find a ride. My family owned only one car for six kids and two parents. After my brother purchased a very nice and expensive bicycle, I imposed upon him to lend it to me when I couldn't get a ride to school. I would pedal the 2.6 miles to school, lock the bike in the bike cage with all the others, and go to class.

On one such day, I returned to the bike cage and was unable to locate the bicycle. The cage easily contained more than fifty bikes, and I spent some time figuring out that the bike was actually gone—I hadn't just forgotten where I locked it up. I slowly realized the bike had been stolen. When I explained to my brother what happened, he was clearly disappointed. He did not blame me, however, and he made no demand of me. He accepted the loss most graciously. Many months later, my federal tax returns arrived in the mail. It amounted to just over two hundred dollars—pretty much exactly what my brother had paid for his bicycle. A few days later, I offered him the cash saying, "Here. Sorry it took so long, but this should make up for losing your bike."

He said, "But it wasn't your fault."

I replied, "But it was my responsibility."

His reaction really surprised me. He sighed heavily. "Thank you. I have been super angry because it didn't seem fair."

I never forgot this experience. I did not feel guilty—I had not done anything wrong. But I did feel something—perhaps it was obligation. And it was this feeling, this sense of justice, that led me to offer the restitution. But I wasn't looking for anything in return, especially forgiveness. My brother was right; it wasn't my fault.

We need different words when we offer restitution so that we can save the language of forgiveness for the use that Jesus intends. We need language that communicates admission of responsibility (not intent) and offers restitution, if possible. "This was a mistake, and I feel badly about it. How can I make it up to you?" We want to help our children cultivate responsibility by teaching them to offer restitution proactively when the situation calls for it. The admission of a mistake and offer of restitution allows us to accept responsibility without confusing our response with contrition. Once the restitution is offered, the damaged party has options: (1) accept the offer, (2) decline the offer, or (3) suggest an alternative.

Let's move now to the forgiveness that Jesus directs us to offer for harm others caused by intent. This forgiveness may involve restitution, but restitution may not be possible. So how does forgiveness work? I found part of my answer in two different mountain ranges.

Many years ago at a very narrow restaurant (literally—it was about fifteen feet wide) in the Sierra Nevada mountains of California, I found the following written on the bathroom wall: "Forgiveness means giving up on hoping for a better yesterday." I thought it was fairly prophetic. It suggests accepting what has happened and moving on. Years later, in the Trinity Mountains of northern California, I was walking along the main street in Weaverville and saw a piece of paper stuck to the inside of a window facing out that simply said this: *How Grace Works: "I forgive you." "I'm sorry."*

This simple construction reveals an important truth. When we teach our children to apologize, we often make them say, "I'm sorry" first, and then we tell them we forgive them. But how powerful would it be to extend the forgiveness first? Then they are free to offer contrition in safety because they know they are already forgiven, not unlike the woman who washes the feet of Jesus. This is the assurance we have from Jesus.

Some years ago I heard a story on National Public Radio (NPR) about a woman named Penny Beerntsen who was raped and later testified at the trial of the accused, a man named Steven Avery. Ultimately, a jury convicted Avery and sent him to prison. Eleven years later, DNA evidence conclusively proved that Avery was, in fact, innocent. Beerntsen was devastated, and she decided to seek out Avery and apologize to him. When she found him, she tried to express the depth of her regret, but Avery responded in a surprising way. "Thank you. But I forgave you a long time ago. You and I are both victims of the same crime."

In the NPR story, Avery forgave Beerntsen, but she wasn't even there when he did it. He did his forgiveness work long before she sought him out. When he said, "I forgave you a long time ago," that seems to mean that he let go of his anger by himself. Her contrition was not necessary; his ability to forgive was not predicated on her guilt or remorse. Through forgiveness, we move from a place of anger or hurt to a place of peace.

Beerntsen might have been able eventually to let go of the guilt without facing the man. After all, she made a mistake but was not seeking to cause intentional harm. Once she understood that he had let go of his anger, perhaps she found letting go of her guilt easier. In both cases, whether expressing forgiveness or contrition, they were reaching for an internal peace.

Prayer

God names prayer as the companion of charity, referring to both as our mutual debt to our neighbor. In *The Dialogue*, God explains that prayer flows from knowledge of God and self and then offers three points of instruction regarding prayer.

First, a person does not succeed in prayer by speaking as many words as possible. God warns Catherine that not much will come from prayer if she prays "only vocally, as do many souls whose prayers are rather words than love. Such as these give heed to nothing except to completing Psalms and saying many paternosters. And when they have once completed their appointed tale, they do not appear to think of anything further, but seem to place devout attention and love in merely vocal recitation . . . which pleases Me but little."[2]

Second, God warns against abandoning words completely. God instructs the soul who wishes to pray to focus its thoughts so that "while she is reciting, she should endeavor to elevate her mind in My love."[3]

Third, prayer as holy desire can be expressed in action as well as thought. God reminds Catherine that "every exercise, whether performed in oneself or in one's neighbor, with goodwill, is prayer."[4]

Jesus also cautions us about the value of words. "Not everyone who says to me 'Lord, Lord,' will enter the kingdom of heaven, but only the one who does the will of my Father in heaven" (Matt. 7:21). Our prayers, however, should not take precedence over our concern for our relationship with our neighbors. "When you are offering your gift at the altar, if you remember that your brother or sister has something against you, leave your gift there before the altar and go; first be reconciled to your brother or sister, and then come and offer your gift" (Matt. 5:23-24).

The Lord's Prayer

As I noted earlier, God encourages Catherine to use the words of prayer to focus her spirit. The prayer Jesus gives us provides a rich practice for the soul. The following table illustrates how each phrase of the Lord's Prayer can serve as a touchstone for the concepts that God shares with Catherine.

The Lord's Prayer		
	Chapter	Connection to the Tree of the Soul
Our Father, who art in heaven, hallowed by thy name.	Chapter Two Chapter Three	*Praise.* You deserve our praise for all things. Holy is your name. *Humility.* We fall on our knees to the Father of Jesus.
Thy kingdom come, thy will be done on earth as it is in heaven.	Chapter Two Chapter Seven Chapter Five Chapter Six	*Wisdom.* Grant us wisdom to understand your will. *Strength.* Grant us courage, persistence, and patience to do your will.
Give us this day our daily bread.	Chapter Three	*Gratitude.* We are wholly dependent on you and grateful for all your blessings.
And forgive us our trespasses, as we forgive those who trespass against us.	Chapter Four Chapter Eight	*Compassion and forgiveness.* Help us offer others the mercy and compassion that you offer us.
And lead us not into temptation, but deliver us from evil.	Chapter One	*Desire.* Grant us freedom from every desire but you.

When we pray the Lord's Prayer, we hold ourselves and others in prayer. When we can't give anything else or when we are unsure how to act, we can always pray.

Sharing Our Faith

The third fruit, sharing our faith, has two components. Sharing may take the form of teaching others about Jesus, or it may involve offering spiritual guidance.

Teaching about Jesus

In chapter five, we focused on understanding—the second power of the soul. God wants us to understand Jesus—his unending mercy, his teachings, and his guidance in our path to God. If we continually reflect upon and deepen this understanding, we will (hopefully) be equipped to share it with others. We never know when we will be called upon to speak on our faith. For me, it happened early in life.

In my freshman year of college, I was blessed—and challenged—with a unique opportunity when someone knocked on the door of my dorm room. I opened it to find a young woman. She said, "I think you are in my theology class." I nodded. She asked, "Can you help me? I don't understand what the professor is talking about. He keeps using a word, and I don't know what it means."

I was not surprised by her request because I was struggling in the class as well. The Jesuit novice who taught the class was using some pretty big words—like *eschatology*—and I was working hard to keep up. "What word?" I asked.

"*Resurrection.*"

I stared at her for a moment. "Did your family go to church when you were younger?" No. "Have you ever read the Bible?" Nope. She truly did not know the story. "Okay, I think I can help you, but we will need some time. Meet me at the library on Sunday at 2:00 p.m. and bring a Bible."

I spent about three hours with her, trying to summarize Judeo-Christian history including the awaiting of the Messiah, the birth and life of Jesus, the Crucifixion, and the Resurrection. I had a hard time because I had more information to share with her than we had time for. I didn't know how to decide what to share and what to leave out. But the most difficult part occurred when I explained the Resurrection. When I talked about Easter morning, her face betrayed her doubt and skepticism. "And you believe that? That Jesus rose . . . from the . . . dead?" In this moment, I experienced my first "profess your faith" opportunity. I hesitated for a second, more due to her reaction than my conviction. But I looked her in the eye, nodded, and quietly said, "I do."

I was only eighteen. I was lucky to have attended a Jesuit high school, where I attended six semesters of theology in four years. Intellectually, I was somewhat prepared. But this sharing meant more than just communicating information. She asked if I *believed.* As we noted earlier, understanding alone does not lead to faith. Faith and reason together can lead to spiritual understanding. In chapter five, we discussed the gift of understanding and its purpose—to understand Jesus—and the necessity of knowing the Gospels well. Here we see again that the Gospels are more than story. We do not merely share a recitation of the gospel story but our belief in Jesus as the Son of God and what that means for our lives.

This fruit of the soul is personal and powerful. It holds great potential for changing lives and for being a force of good in the world. The conviction of our faith creates a strong and compelling gift we can share with others. We can help make disciples of all nations.

Spiritual Direction

Spiritual direction gets only a brief mention in the tree of the soul, listed as one of the fruits along with charity. But later in *The Dialogue*, God talks at length about spiritual counseling and cautions Catherine about the following: (1) naming the sins of others too directly, (2) being judgmental of others, and (3) insisting others follow her spiritual path.[5] This instruction reveals three simple rules to follow when giving spiritual direction to others: encourage good instead of labeling bad, replace judgment with compassion, and let others follow their own spiritual paths.

God directs Catherine not to confront people with specific sins or failures but instead to "let silence or a holy argument for virtue be in your mouth to discourage vice."[6] Paul's letter to the Ephesians provides similar advice. It suggests that our words should be "useful for building up, as there is need, so that your words may give grace to those who hear" (Eph. 4:29). As we have learned from decades of psychological research, rewarding good behavior proves more effective than punishing bad behavior. God's teachings are centuries ahead of modern psychology.

The humble soul admits what it does not know. In particular, it cannot know the intentions of others. No one can judge the hidden heart but God alone. We must avoid the temptation of playing judge over other people's intentions and remind ourselves that our neighbor's plight could someday be our own. This well-known adage succinctly expresses the sentiment: There but for the grace of God go I. Jesus encourages us to focus on growing in our own self-knowledge without harping on others. In the Gospel of Matthew, Jesus asks us, "Why do you see the speck in your neighbor's eye, but do not notice the log in your own eye?" (7:3). With regard to the spiritual guidance of others, we choose to focus on compassion instead of judgment.

When we assume that our spiritual path is the only one, we act in opposition to humility to which God calls us. Claiming that we have it all figured out sets us up to lead our neighbor instead of traveling with him or her. We are all on this journey together, all climbing the proverbial holy mountain. God reminds Catherine that our path is not the only one. It is not our place to say to anyone, "Follow me."

The Example of a Holy Life

Even after working through a time of discernment, the path forward may still be unclear. We may not be sure how we should act, or we may realize that others' needs exceed our ability to fix them. When we see others struggling, we must remember that we can offer "the edification of a holy and honorable life."[7] What does that mean?

We are each created in God's image, and when we let God's presence shine through us, we become a source of grace for others. God tells Catherine that each of us has different gifts in varying degrees—no one has all the virtues. So we needn't develop a list of attributes specifying what it means to live a holy life. Upon reflection, I believe the best way to approach this topic is to share stories about three people who have demonstrated for me what it means to live a holy life. One is someone I worked with professionally, one is a family member, and one is a dear friend. None of these folks is perfect. But they are precious to me because the virtues I see in them have provided not only a model for me but also inspiration.

Peace and Courage

I met Sister Marian Clare Valenteen, RSM, in 2003. The bishop of the Catholic Diocese of Stockton invited her to serve as superintendent of schools when I was the assistant superintendent. We quickly became friends, and although I see her less often now than I would like, the impact of her presence in my life has not changed.

I detect two overarching qualities in my friend Clare. The first is her sense of peace. She brings calmness and tranquility with her when she walks into the room. Don't get me wrong, she can get agitated just like anybody, but her natural state is peace, like the calm waters of a lake or a gentle waterfall. After spending time with her, I leave calmer than when I came. I believe this to be the direct result of a rich prayer life and a lifetime of devotion to God.

Clare's second quality is the virtue of courage. As the superintendent, she faced some tough issues, including the closing of one of our schools—a trying matter for everyone in a school community. Staff felt rejected and parents felt abandoned. To these contentious conversations, Clare brought her calmness, but she also brought a resolve of steel. She worked through hard conversations with parish pastors, staff, and parents, and she did not back down from any challenging task. At the same time, she never let the difficulty of the situation rob her of that greater sense of peace that she carried with her. When I describe her to other people, one of the very first things I say is, "You should meet my friend Clare because the lady just radiates grace."

Patience and Humility

My model for both of these virtues is a relative, who—humbly—asked not to be named. This soul portrays the very definition of humility. This relative of mine is unassuming, never asking for anything personally. Instead, this good soul continues to dedicate each day to the service of family. This family member shies away from recognition for generosity and never seeks personal attention. If someone offers a compliment, my relative will offer a simple thanks, and then the conversation will quickly turn to another topic, often to point out others who deserve credit or thanks.

My family member accompanies this humility with an astounding amount of patience. All my life, I have watched this person practice this virtue, particularly in difficult situations. Almost never reacting out of anger or frustration, this role model pauses with grace, taking time to think before responding. If someone comes to this person for help after making a big mistake, he or she should not expect a lecture. Instead, this model of patience and humility is more likely to gently say, "I'll help you any way I can."

Joy and Purity

I have been friends with Teresa for more than thirty years. We met when I was seventeen, and we worked together at a summer camp. We have remained friends ever since. Teresa has many endearing qualities, but two stand out for me. The first is her capacity for joy. She can be truly glad for others' good fortune. The smile on her face and the sound of her voice show me that her happiness for others is deep and genuine. When Teresa is happy for me, her wonderfully infectious laughter actually increases my own happiness.

Her second quality is the virtue of purity. In many ways, she serves as my standard for that term. Her thoughts are drawn to goodness and light and what is best in others. Being hurtful or mean is simply not her nature. When Jesus says, "Blessed are the pure in heart, for they will see God" (Matt. 5:8), I believe he means people like Teresa.

All three of my spiritual models share one common trait: They remain committed to their faith. They live the gospel in ways that are plain for all to see. It is so integrated into who they are that they need not explain what they believe. By watching their words and actions, we know. I have benefited greatly from all three. I am a better person because I know them and because I witness their powerful examples of a holy life.

Summary

- God specifically mentions four fruits of the tree of the soul: charity, prayer, sharing our faith, and the example of a holy life.
- Charity is the queen of the virtues. Being charitable includes showing forgiveness.
- Together, prayer and charity constitute our "mutual debt to our neighbor."
- Sharing our faith means helping others understand Jesus and offering spiritual direction characterized by encouragement and a lack of judgment.
- When we feel as if we have nothing to offer others, we can always offer the example of a holy life.

Prayer

In prayer, reflect with God on your recent choices and on your opportunities to practice charity, forgiveness, teaching, and spiritual direction. Ask for the grace to see where your fruits are most needed.

> *God, as I begin this day, help me to be mindful of the people around me. Grant me the grace to see their needs and to serve as a humble source of charity, forgiveness, teaching, and spiritual direction according to your will. Let the example of my life strengthen others in faith and virtue. Help me to bear good fruit today. Amen.*

For Reflection

Who in your life needs charity from you? With whom do you need to reconcile? How can you work toward letting go of your anger or hurt? Who in your life needs spiritual direction? (It may be you!) Who are your role models for a holy life? What qualities make them holy for you? What virtues do they exemplify?

PART V

PERSONAL PRACTICE

The tree of the soul provides a framework for Christian spiritual growth. The symbol of the tree and its different parts help us remember how key Christian virtues work together in our souls. The top of the tree reminds us that the fruit that should come from our spiritual work is charity, prayer, and help for our neighbors in need. The trunk of the tree reminds us what makes us strong—the three powers of memory, understanding, and will, along with the virtues of patience, persistence, and courage. The roots and soil remind us that the Christian soul grounds itself in humility and the law of compassion.

The circle on the ground—the space in which the tree grows—becomes wider and deeper through knowledge of self and of God.

We may feel compelled to focus our spiritual growth at the top of the tree, to concentrate our efforts on action alone. True, we must bring the virtues to birth through action, but the action must flow from humility and love. God tells Catherine that all our acts are finite. The love of God, though, is infinite. God instructs Catherine to seek a holy life by making the intent of her heart pure and unselfish. That can only be achieved through deep and consistent self-exploration.

The significant work of knowing ourselves and God can bring us to a place of humility and compassion. We are the gardeners of the tree of our soul. No other person can increase the size and depth of the circle in which our tree must grow. We must do it. Through the Holy Spirit's guidance, we can fill that space with the soil of humility and establish the roots of compassion.

We focus on this work through our self-reflection, meditation, and prayer. Only by working internally—by knowing ourselves and knowing God—can we learn to recognize the emotions, thoughts, and desires that move us away from God. When we have recognized these in ourselves, we can more freely accept the gift that Jesus offers: an abundant life full of joy.

In the World

An internal spiritual practice focused on self-knowledge and knowledge of God will reward us. But we also have to be aware of what is going on around us externally. Sometimes our daily life can seem ordinary. Other times we are confronted with challenges, and we may not know how to respond. At these times, we can apply what we have learned through the tree of the soul. The process outlined below combines each aspect of the tree of the soul into a single process.

Knowing Self

- As I consider a particular matter, what emotions do I feel?
- What adjectives or labels am I applying to other people?
- What do I want?

Knowing God

- What do scripture and prayer reveal to me about this matter?
- What gifts do I have to offer? What gifts do others have to offer?
- How can my response strengthen or draw upon the faith community?
- What service is needed?

Humility

- In what ways am I judging others? demonstrating gratitude for the good I have received? assuming my perceptions are the whole truth and ignoring what others are experiencing?

Compassion

- To what extent am I seeing the suffering or need of others? willing to help without reward or recognition? willing to help everyone in need equally?

Three Powers

- How am I showing gratefulness for blessings I have received that others may need? reflecting on the depth of Jesus' love for me? allowing God's wisdom to direct my will?

Three Virtues

- To what extent am I demonstrating patience by treating others pleasantly? demonstrating persistence by giving the matter time and effort? demonstrating courage by not shrinking away from a difficult, uncomfortable, or scary situation?

Discernment

- To what extent am I acting calmly? seeking the counsel of others? acting with integrity?

Fruits

- What action(s) demonstrate compassion as an expression of God's goodness and mercy?
- How is charity needed?
- How can I pray for those involved?
- What teaching or guidance can I offer?
- What example can I show others?

EPILOGUE

I have spent several years in the company of Catherine of Siena's tree of the soul. As I conclude this study, I am looking out the window at a midwinter morning. After a warm February seduced many trees into an early bloom, March has begun to reassert winter's claim. A great storm is moving across northern California, promising a few feet of snow for the mountains and flash flood warnings in the valleys and coastlines. Some trees will fall due to the wind and rain-drenched soil, but most won't. Most trees endure. Trees are strong—as is the soul.

We all have the capacity to survive the winds of adversity, parts of life which we unfortunately cannot avoid. We may not begin our lives as sequoias, but we can grow spiritually over time and thrive despite life's challenges. God's metaphor of the tree reveals the necessity of being deeply rooted. When we invest in the health of our soil and the depth and strength of our roots, our souls will grow and remain strong. By focusing our awareness on knowing ourselves and God, by looking at the world through the lens of humility and compassion, and by letting the powers and virtues of the soul guide our daily living, we can yield the fruit that Jesus promises.

APPENDIX A
THE TREE OF THE SOUL

The following paragraphs from *The Dialogue*, translated by Algar Thorold in 1907, served as inspiration for this book.*

Do you know how these three virtues stand together? It is, as if a circle were drawn on the surface of the earth, and a tree, with an off-shoot joined to its side, grew in the center of the circle. The tree is nourished in the earth contained in the diameter of the circle, for if the tree were out of the earth it would die, and give no fruit. Now, consider, in the same way, that the soul is a tree existing by love, and that it can live by nothing else than love; and, that if this soul have not in very truth the divine love of perfect charity, she cannot produce the fruit of life, but only of death. It is necessary then, that the root of this tree, that is the affection of the soul, should grow in, and issue from the circle of true self-knowledge which is contained in Me, who have neither beginning nor end, like the circumference of the circle, for, turn as you will within a circle, inasmuch as the circumference has neither end nor beginning, you always remain within it.

This knowledge of yourself and of Me is found in the earth of true humility, which is as wide as the diameter of the circle, that is, as the knowledge of self and of Me (for, otherwise, the circle would not be without end and beginning, but would have its beginning in knowledge of self, and its end in confusion, if this knowledge were not contained in Me). Then the tree of love feeds itself on humility, bringing forth from its side the off-shoot of true discretion, in the way that I have already told you, from the heart of the tree, that is the affection of love which is in the soul, and the patience, which proves that I am in the soul and the soul in Me. This tree then, so sweetly planted, produces fragrant blossoms of virtue, with many scents of great variety, inasmuch as the soul renders fruit of grace and of utility to her neighbor, according to the zeal of those who come to receive fruit from My servants; and to Me she renders the sweet odor of glory and praise to My Name, and so fulfills the object of her creation.

*Catherine of Siena, *The Dialogue of the Seraphic Virgin Catherine of Siena*, trans. Algar Thorold (London: Kegan, Paul, Trench, Trubner & Co., Ltd., 1907), 25–26.

APPENDIX B
SUGGESTIONS FOR GROUP
FACILITATORS

Being asked to serve as a group facilitator may cause some anxiety, but many find the role enjoyable and rewarding. With a little bit of thought and preparation, you can help make your small group's discussions meaningful. Your group may not *need* strong facilitation, but even highly cohesive small groups can benefit from a facilitator. Also, while people who volunteer to facilitate faith-sharing groups often host them as well, the two roles can be separated and performed by different people.

The Facilitator's Role

The purpose of group study is to learn from others by sharing experiences. Sharing your spiritual journey and faith can feel personal and vulnerable. It requires trust, gentleness, patience, and respect from all the participants. As a facilitator of a group study, your role is to help create the conditions that will enhance the ability of everyone to participate. You can do that by attending to four important matters: comfort, structure, culture, and engagement.

Comfort

Work with the host to ensure that the gathering place is well-suited to the group's needs. If you meet in a private home, any living or family room will usually work as long as there is a comfortable seat for every participant. Many participants enjoy having a table where they can write and take notes if that's possible. If there are participants who need walking support (canes, walkers, or wheelchairs), allow for clear pathways in the space. Remember that participants may need access to a restroom and water. Finally, be mindful of the temperature and lighting.

Structure

Provide structure by using a consistent agenda for each gathering, establishing simple ground rules, and enforcing them with a gentle hand. A consistent agenda or outline helps participants know what to expect. Ground rules build confidence among participants that the conversation will be balanced.

Culture

As a facilitator, you want to help create a group study experience that is meaningful. As you prepare for your leadership role, consider the following ideas.

Explore. Understanding the experience of others requires more than just listening. Take time to ask clarifying questions such as *How did it make you feel at the time?*, *How do you see it now looking back?*, and *How did it affect your faith?*

Don't rush. Offer yourself and your small group the time to work thoughtfully and purposefully. Covering all the material is *not* the goal. Giving the group members an opportunity to contribute as they wish and to talk about things that matter to them is more important. If your group spends the whole session on a single idea, that's okay.

Guide, not teach. A good description for a facilitator is "guide on the side" and not "sage on the stage." The role of the facilitator is not to teach but to guide the participants in a productive way by using open-ended questions and helping people bridge ideas. Be careful not to give answers. The model is retreat, not classroom.

Engagement

Keep the conversation moving. If one question doesn't get much traction, suggest that the group move to a different question. However, a thoughtful, quiet moment offers participants a chance to collect their thoughts. If the silence begins to feel uncomfortable or awkward, take action.

Model the participation you want to see. Whatever you ask the group to do, you must be willing to do as well. Be prepared to answer a question first if participants are slow to start. But always remember that facilitators don't lecture or teach. Instead, they offer ideas to start group discussion.

Balance the input. When others do engage, you may need to encourage the quieter people when appropriate and slow down the more verbal members of the group if necessary.

A Word about Food

Sharing a meal can be a powerful part of sharing faith. Like Martha, I feel compelled to offer refreshments to guests when they enter my home. Whenever my friends or family show up at my door, I always ask, "Would you like something to drink?" My need to offer food to those who enter my home doesn't change simply because a group is gathering to discuss matters of faith.

That said, faith-sharing can be easily diverted by combining the session with a meal. If your group meets in a private home, staging a meal could place a burden upon the host. If the group decides that it wants to include meals, be sure to plan extra time for managing the preparation, serving, and cleanup involved with the meal. This could substantially increase the amount of time necessary for the group meeting.

Another option is to forgo a full meal and instead have a simple snack or possibly dessert, depending on the time of day. Some groups prefer to start with community building first, with a specific end time for the gathering. Other groups choose to end with light refreshment, which can help the participants transition from faith-sharing to a lighter, social context before they depart. If meetings run long, the host can signal the end is near by bringing out the snack.

Before the First Meeting

- With the host, establish the location, dates, and times for the group study, and share those with all participants.
- Clarify which pages of the book participants should read in advance.
- Remind participants to bring their copy of *Deeply Rooted*, a Bible, notebook, and pen.
- Complete the assigned reading.
- Arrive in time for any last minute preparation you may need.

The First Meeting

Whenever a group convenes for the first time, you must attend to some basic hospitality and logistical details.

Introductions. Find out how each person prefers to be addressed. Consider providing name tags for the first few meetings. You might go around the room and ask participants to introduce themselves briefly.

Communication. Clarify how participants can communicate with you and the host outside of meetings.

Comfort. Point out the restroom and kitchen, if you will be serving food.

Ground rules. Successful groups have a clear understanding of the rules for participating in discussion. Ground rules often include agreeing to arrive on time, doing the advance reading and preparation, and interacting respectfully.

Sample Ground Rules

- We start on time with prayer.
- We let everyone participate; no one dominates the conversation.
- We avoid interrupting one another.
- We don't judge or criticize other people's experience.
- We hold one another's words and stories in confidence.
- We end on time with prayer.

Discussion can be slow to start, especially if participants don't know one another. If you're having trouble getting people talking, here are two strategies to try.

Short, silent reflection. Not everyone always has time to do the reading, and some people need a refresher on the information before jumping into deep discussions. After the opening prayer, you could say, "I know all of you have read the material, but it's been a long week. Why don't we take a few minutes to scan the content and refresh our memory?"

Quick answer. Ask each person to describe briefly an idea, concept, or topic that he or she would like to discuss and share with the group. This method gets everyone talking, creates energy in the room, and surfaces common areas of interest for discussion.

Outline for Group Discussion

1. Begin with prayer. You can make up your own or use the sample prayers at the end of each chapter.

2. Use these general questions to start the conversation.

    • What inspired you? bothered you? confused you?
    • At what points did you disagree with the author?
    • What events in your life connect to the ideas in this chapter?

3. Use the specific questions for the chapter being discussed.

4. Call for a closing prayer when you are within five minutes of the end time.

5. Remind everyone of the time, place, and content for the next meeting. You might also remind them to do the following:

    • Review the *For Reflection* section at the end of the chapter.
    • Connect the content to what's going on in your life. Write down your ideas and thoughts throughout the week.
    • Pray for the group.

Chapter One: Knowing Self

- The author suggests knowing yourself is an important step in the process of knowing God. How difficult is it for you to focus on yourself in this way?
- The author introduces three aspects of self-knowledge: your feelings, thoughts, and attachments. Which of these do you know best about yourself? Which of these is hardest to know about yourself?
- What other aspects of the self are not covered by these three categories?
- The author proposes six truths about feelings. Consider a recent event when your feelings obstructed your ability to see clearly. Looking back, what role did these six truths play in your situation?
- What labels do you assign to other people? Think about persons you saw today. What assumptions did you make about them?
- If you catch yourself having thoughts that you know you should not pursue, how do you get rid of them?
- Think of an attachment—something that makes you happy and that you would not want to lose. With that in mind, describe a time when you were happy before that attachment came into your life. How were you able to be happy without this attachment?

Chapter Two: Knowing God

- The author introduces four premises to ground us in our efforts to know God.

- *God is transcendent.* Discuss the need to admit what we do not know about God. Outside of scripture and Jesus, what symbolizes the Divine for you?
- *God is beyond our vocabulary.* How can silence become a part of your spiritual practice. How can you silence not only the mouth but also the mind?
- *We are more than mind and body.* How do you love God with all your mind and soul? How is reality more than what your senses detect and your mind understands? Share a time when you experienced a flash of revelation or a surge of inspired faith.
- *God is immanent.* How are you created in God's likeness?

Chapter Three: Humility

- The author introduces four characteristics of humility.
  - *Praise.* What form of praise fills you with the Spirit?
  - *Patience.* What pushes your buttons and tries your patience? When you lose your patience, who is often the victim?
  - *Gratefulness.* Whom or what do you take for granted? How do you offer thanks to God?
  - *Lack of judgment.* About what matters are you quick to judge? Who in your life deserves a nonjudgmental response from you?
- Who is your model of humility?
- The author suggests that humility requires you to accept that someone else's experience is as valid as your own. How can you set aside your own assumption that you perceive things accurately?

Chapter Four: Compassion

- The author describes his daughter's reaction to the plight of a homeless person. When you encounter homelessness, how do you react?
- Describe a time when you felt compassion toward a stranger or a family member.
- Discuss an experience of wanting to help but being unable to do so.
- What experiences evoke the greatest compassion in you?
- When have you been on the receiving end of compassion when it was unexpected or desperately needed?

Chapter Five: Powers of the Soul

- How have you experienced the winds of prosperity, adversity, fear, and conscience?
- God gives Catherine a different interpretation of the phrase of "where two or three are gathered in my name." Discuss your reactions to the *two* referring to the two great laws and the *three* referring to the powers of the soul.
- Memory gives us the ability to recall the blessings to our soul. Share with the group a powerful spiritual memory. How often do you actively recall that memory? How would your life change if you remembered it every day?
- The purpose of understanding is to contemplate the depth of God's love revealed in Jesus. Do you struggle with understanding God's love? If so, who in your life gives you a glimpse of God's love for you?
- Discuss the difficulty in moving beyond intellectual understanding.

- God tells Catherine that the will—our freedom to choose—leads to suffering. Identify a time when your suffering or unhappiness was the result of a choice you made.
- When has your freedom been compromised by strong desire?
- When has your reason been constrained by strong emotion? Have you ever been so angry that you acted irrationally?
- Exercising the will requires action. Sometimes we have noble thoughts—good ideas for helping others—but we don't act on them. Why?
- What drains your willpower?

Chapter Six: Virtues of the Soul

- Who in your life exemplifies the virtue of patience?
- When have you succumbed to your impatience?
- Describe a time when persistence paid off in your life.
- What part of life or faith requires the most courage from you right now? What difficulty or disappointment are you facing?

Chapter Seven: Discernment

- How do you calm yourself when you are angry, upset, or not at peace?
- What sources have you used to help you in the discernment process? Who is the Solomon you go to when you need perspective? Share an example of the wisdom you received by asking someone else.
- How important is integrity to you? What would happen if you made a decision that was inconsistent with what you

profess to believe? How would it affect your friends and family?

Chapter Eight: Fruits of the Soul

- When was the last time you bore the following fruits: charity (including forgiveness), prayer, sharing your faith, living a holy life?
- Which of these fruits do you experience the most often?
- Which, if any, of the fruits are easier to enact than others? Why?

NOTES

From the Desk of Catherine of Siena

1. Catherine of Siena, *The Dialogue of the Seraphic Virgin Catherine of Siena*, trans. Algar Thorold (London: Kegan, Paul, Trench, Trubner & Co., Ltd., 1907). This work was scanned and edited by Harry Plantinga in 1994 and can be found at http://www.catholicplanet.com/ebooks/Dialogue-of-St-Catherine.pdf.
2. Catherine of Siena, *Catherine of Siena: The Dialogue*, trans. Suzanne Noffke, O.P. (New York: Paulist Press, 1980), 3–7.

The Tree at a Glance

1. Noffke, *Catherine of Siena*, 102.

Part I: The Garden

1. Thorold, *The Dialogue*, 16.

Chapter One: Knowing Self

1. Catherine of Siena, *Saint Catherine of Siena as Seen in Her Letters*, trans. and ed. Vida Dutton Scudder (London: J. M. Dent and E. P. Dutton, 1905). This work was scanned by Project Gutenburg and can be found at http://onlinebooks.library.upenn.edu/webbin/gutbook/lookup?num=7403.
2. Thorold, *The Dialogue*, 56.
3. Ibid., 35.
4. Raimon Panikkar, *The Rhythm of Being: The Unbroken Trinity* (Maryknoll, NY: Orbis Books, 2013), 144.

5. Anthony de Mello, *Awareness: A de Mello Spirituality Conference in His Own Words*, ed. J. Francis Stroud, S.J. (New York: Image Books, 1992), 173.
6. Thorold, *The Dialogue*, 16.

Chapter Two: Knowing God

1. Noffke, *Catherine of Siena*, 184.
2. Panikkar, *The Rhythm of Being*, 10.
3. Thorold, *The Dialogue*, 41.
4. Ibid., 14.

Chapter Three: Humility

1. Thorold, *The Dialogue*, 24.
2. Ibid.
3. Ibid., 125.
4. Ibid., 20.
5. Ibid., 25.
6. Ibid., 117.
7. Ibid., 41.

Chapter Four: Compassion

1. Thorold, *The Dialogue*, 59.
2. Noffke, *Catherine of Siena*, 114.

Chapter Five: Powers of the Soul

1. Noffke, *Catherine of Siena*, 174.
2. Thorold, *The Dialogue*, 54.
3. Ibid., 56.
4. Noffke, *Catherine of Siena*, 108.
5. George MacDonald, *Your Life in Christ: The Nature of God and His Work in Human Hearts*, ed. Michael Phillips (Minneapolis, MN: Bethany House Publishers, 2005), 58–59.
6. Thorold, *The Dialogue*, 35.
7. Ibid., 56.
8. Ibid.
9. Ibid., 54.
10. Ibid., 59.

11. Ibid., 110.
12. Ibid., 38.
13. Ibid., 107.
14. Ibid., 56.
15. Ibid., 50.
16. Ibid., 36.

Chapter Six: Virtues of the Soul

1. Thorold, *The Dialogue*, 19.
2. Ibid., 22.
3. Ibid., 58.
4. Ibid., 53.
5. Ibid., 39.

Chapter Seven: Discernment

1. Noffke, *Catherine of Siena*, 42.
2. Thorold, *The Dialogue*, 28.

Chapter Eight: Fruits of the Soul

1. Thorold, *The Dialogue*, 21.
2. Ibid., 68.
3. Ibid.
4. Ibid., 70.
5. Noffke, *Catherine of Siena*, 193–96.
6. Ibid., 194.
7. Thorold, *The Dialogue*, 22.

CPSIA information can be obtained at www.ICGtesting.com
Printed in the USA
LVOW10s0320150616

492632LV00001B/1/P